48067

1.

31.

THE SCOTTISH ISLANDS

1 The Bass Rock

THE
SCOTTISH
ISLANDS

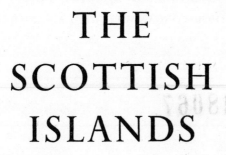

George
Scott-Moncrieff

LONDON
B. T. BATSFORD LTD

TO NEIL AND DOROTHY USHER

FOR THEIR LONGANIMITY WITH MY INSULARITY.

48067

914.1

First published 1952

MADE AND PRINTED IN GREAT BRITAIN BY
WILLIAM CLOWES AND SONS, LIMITED, LONDON AND BECCLES, FOR THE PUBLISHERS
B. T. BATSFORD, LTD.
LONDON: 15 NORTH AUDLEY STREET, W.1 AND MALVERN WELLS, WORCESTERSHIRE
NEW YORK: 122 EAST 55TH STREET   TORONTO: 103 ST. CLAIR AVENUE WEST
SYDNEY: 156 CASTLEREAGH STREET

CONTENTS

LIST OF ILLUSTRATIONS

INTRODUCTION

THE land area of the four main groups of the islands of Scotland may be divided into seven parts. The Inner Hebrides account for three of these, the Outer Hebrides for two, and Orkney and Shetland for one each. On these divisions I have based the general proportions of my book with one additional chapter for the other isles and a brief conclusion. Within the separate divisions all is arbitrary, depending upon personal predilection, whim, familiarity, and loquacity, in varying degrees.

There seem to be countless things that I could have said and have not, largely for restriction of space. Nor have I any conviction that the things I have said were the most worth saying, interesting, or important, but can only hope that in their sum they may provide something of a general picture of the isles sauced with the particular of one man's viewpoint.

There must be very few people who know a lot of the islands intimately. There are a great many of them, and life is short. Persons generally tend to know one island, or one group, to the exclusion of the others. Although I have at one time or another visited all the larger and a number of the lesser isles, and have lived on two and made repeated stays on others, there are big gaps in my knowledge, and, particularly, in my intimacy. Yet, much as the islands differ in themselves, they have important things in common. I suppose one first is drawn to islands by the romance of their small dominion, their narrow separation from the sea, some element of escape—no bad thing—from a too jostling, complicated mainland. Many have great æsthetic appeal such as the more crowded parts of Britain have, unfortunately, long been losing. One is inspired to linger, or to stay, for additional reasons: not least, the people. It is very wholesome, the company of persons relatively free from so much of the contemporary confusion of mind.

Although no doubt it might be analysed more precisely, I have referred to this contemporary confusion as being the spirit of the Industrial Age. Faced with the native islesfolk, one experiences a sense of guilt, something like that which many of us feel when first faced with the upbringing of small children, in appreciating simplicity, an innate innocence, in their responses which makes one realise that one has as much, at least, to learn from as to teach them. In comparison with the trivial points of technique and commerce that islanders might learn from the bigger world, and perhaps learn too often without advantage, I think they have incomparably more important things to teach. Only, perhaps, the lesson is not very easy to instil: not mass-produced nor for mass-consumption. I think it concerns, at its core, some quality of intuitive living which contemporary education, while it may often smother, almost totally ignores. Mr. Aldous Huxley has remarked that modern education merely gives distractions to those who formerly were free from them. It certainly develops a faculty which in many individual cases may be very weak, and better left undeveloped than stimulated at the expense of one that is very distinct and every bit as important.

However, I am not concerned to argue this abstruse point either here or in the ensuing pages, which are concerned primarily with presenting some fine bits of the world to those who may visit or think of visiting them. It would, however, be discourteous not to speak of those other people who are our hosts there, nor to say a word in their defence when, small minority as they are, their way of life is so discountenanced, occasionally viciously, generally out of sheer stupidity.

If I have written with acerbity of some Governmental efforts to redress the balance, it is not that I overlook the excellent jobs done by many individual officials, but only that I am afraid that general administrative policy in Britain is based upon that series of misconceptions that I have loosely dubbed as appertaining to the Industrial Age, and which, in the long run, cannot but continue the depopulation of the isles, the drift to exterminate good peoples and ways of life.

GEORGE SCOTT-MONCRIEFF

2 The Island of Staffa

From an early Victorian Lithograph

THE INNER HEBRIDES

I

ISLAY is the southernmost of the Hebridean Islands. It is true that Arran is sometimes claimed as being of the Hebrides, but, lying as it does in the landlocked waters between the Mull of Kintyre and the Ayrshire mainland, Arran is separated from the true Hebridean chain that stretches from the Oa of Islay to the Butt of Lewis, with St. Kilda and North Rona remote dependencies to west and north. The Hebrides themselves divide naturally into the Inner Isles and the Outer Isles. Of these the inner group stretch the farther and have the larger area of land.

Islay is not particularly typical of the Hebrides, if, indeed, the great variety of these islands admits of any emphatic peculiarity of type. It is rather Lowland in character. Much of it is very green: but, although there is good arable land, the green is a little deceptive, often covering thin soil above deep deposits of peat. This peat is very important to Islay. Along that astonishing seven-mile streak of straight level road, so unusual for Scotland, that covers most of the distance between Port Ellen in the south and Bowmore, the old capital in the centre of the island, the green skin is peeled from the black peat-beds and great quantities of peats lifted for the distilleries of famous, thirsty names: Laphroaig, Ardbeg, Lagavulin. Islay is the chief home of whisky of West Highland Type: a heavy, strong-flavoured whisky, the malt prepared over sweet-scented fires of pure peat.

Port Ellen, on the southern seaboard, is now the most important of the Islay townships. The steamer calls there on alternate days, lying overnight and sailing for Tarbert in the morning. The steamer company have erected a hideous box of an office on the pier, otherwise the little town is chiefly attractive, rather Gallovidian in character, neat, painted houses, with a general gentle untidiness. A ring of houses confronts the bay in a comely curve. The harbour is good, with a natural breakwater formed by rocks and reefs running out from the little headland of the Ard. It opens out into a larger bay, the far side bright with golden sands. The sands can be approached along rocks hard and secure for clambering only with that slight inexplicable sense of imperfect cleanliness of all seaboards that are not remote from human habitation, unlike most Hebridean shores. They are good sands: behind them a large graveyard around one of the innumerable ruined pre-Reformation churches of the Hebrides. From within the fragmentary walls a fine knight in armour and an angel look up unexpectedly. A separate enclosure hains the bodies washed up on Islay when the *Tuscania* was sunk in 1918, now joined by those of sailors of the Second World War.

The road east from Port Ellen runs, by way of distilleries, to the woods of Kildalton. Here is another ruined church, more complete, and near it a noble cross, ringed with an open wheel in the Celtic manner, carved in high relief. This road ends in another bay, remote and clean, facing east to the mainland. North of it there is hilly country, rising to 1,600 feet, in reality a lopped-off continuation of the mountains of Jura across the Sound of Islay. It is this hilly country that one sees when approaching Islay by air from the mainland, dark moorland uncharacteristic of most of the island, scarred by watercourses. The plane comes down at Glenegedale on the links above the huge stretch of sand along Laggan Bay. Here all is green: wonderful springy turf of the kind that inspired the invention of golf and must make any golfer's fingers twitch. But during the late war the airport turf was replaced by dull grey asphalt runways, far more costly and difficult to maintain.

Round the promontory to the north of Laggan Bay the sea runs into Lochindaal, a deep bight that goes near to joining Loch Gruineart and cutting Islay into two islands. It is an enclosed and

3 Volcanic landscape, the Quiraing, Isle of Skye

4 Houses in a Tiree crofting village

5 Old style Tiree house, modernised with a felt roof replacing the thatch

6. The Round Church in the Islay township of Bowmore,
laid out in the eighteenth century

sluggish sea, a wide plain bay from which the tide recedes to bare sea-mud wrinkled with the casts of millions of lugworms: a sea too lazy to carry away the silt that now impedes activity at the pier of Bowmore. Along the straighter coast opposite, the water has a clearer run, and here the enterprising lobster-fishermen of Port Charlotte have lately built their own pier, working neck-deep in water to do so.

Up from the Bowmore pier a wide street leads to the top of the slope which is crowned with a delightful kirk. It is a round kirk, its walls harled and kept nicely whitewashed, fronted on the seaward side by a pleasant steeple of grey stone stepped back to a small stone dome (6). Above the door is a florid Latin inscription, telling that the kirk was built in 1767 by the Campbell lord of the island. The adjacent houses date from the ensuing years, rather earlier than those at Port Ellen, of a pleasant Lowland character such as one might expect on the domain of a laird bent upon developing his property at that period. Chiefly they are painted, with door and window jambs picked out in contrasting colours, wide-gabled comfortable houses proclaiming civilisedness and gentility in sharp distinction to the rash of prefabs that have erupted beyond the kirk. (The prefabs compare unfavourably with the oil-stores put up during the war on the other side of the kirk and never used.)

Islay had become a Campbell possession in 1615 during the period when James VI was actively and successfully subduing the violence of the island chiefs. The island had always been a rich and important possession, the home of the Lords of the Isles, a title ultimately annexed to the Crown in 1540. The later Islay MacDonalds remained intransigent. On the long strand of Traigh Gruineart they fought one of the bloodiest of all the clan battles, repelling, with great slaughter, an attempt by Macleans from Mull to lay claim to the Rhinns of Islay. Their home was the Castle of Dunyvaig and they were known as the Lords of Dunyvaig and the Glens, for they had large possessions in Ulster. It was the Campbells who made Islay House their home and bestowed their daughters' names on Port Ellen and Port Charlotte. The successful campaigns of the Earls of Argyle for long assured that the southern isles of the Inner Hebrides, and also the adjacent mainland, were possessed by, or under the superiority of, the clan. Of all the once great MacDonald possessions only the little island of Cara, with the property of Largie on the neighbouring Kintyre coast, remained, as it still does remain, with a cadet family of the Lords of the Isles.

Islay House stands a little north of Bowmore, above the saltings at the head of Lochindaal. It is a substantial mansion, much altered and added to, but given some unity and attraction by the white harling of its walls. Being in a sheltered part, its policies are finely wooded with well-grown trees, unlike the wind-combed clumps to be seen along the Rhinns. Beside it the road forks right for Port Askaig.

Port Askaig is the northern port, served alternately with Port Ellen, the two being connected by a bus service. Approaching it, the country is more broken and interesting than much of Islay. I remember a first view of the Paps of Jura seen when walking along the Port Askaig road, the tops rising through broken white cloud like blankets tumbled about them. Then swiftly the clouds fell apart, revealing the lovely shapely peaks, aptly named. Mostly one sees only two of them, but there are, unnaturally, three Paps of Jura. They form a cloud-trap and are constantly changing with mists gathering and dispersing, mournful in shadow, then suddenly rejoicing in sunshine.

Port Askaig is very different from Port Ellen. One winds down on to it through woods, finding it suddenly at one's feet: half a dozen white houses, a little pier, the bright dark blue waters of the Sound of Islay swirling past, one little white house visible on the Jura shore. The clachan is built along a narrow flat ledge bounded to north and south by rocks tree-surmounted. To the south are the policies of Dunlossit House, a wonderful sight in early summer with their forests of rhododendrons: masses and masses of purple-flowering ponticum in clumps and avenues and jungles. They enfold two little lochs, and always beyond them flows the bright water of the Sound. The shore is formed of a low cliff, broken rocks of much variety, accessible by paths and tracks.

North along the Sound from Port Askaig are two more large white distilleries, Caol Ila and Bonahaven. Each has its own little pier, making it independent of the rough road along the top of the cliff. Even today there is a surprising lot of traffic along the Sound, vessels of all kinds and sizes passing up and down with agreeable, independent busy-ness. The people at the ferry remember when it was far busier though: "You had to be careful that you weren't run down taking the ferry across." One imagines it then a sort of liquid Sauchiehall Street. The ferryman's sister has a story of herself hearing, on a black-out night of the '39 war, a crying out in the little bay, "just like a child, it was". They had newly had word of a big ship torpedoed off the coast. She fetched a flashlight and a clean towel and went along the beach, the crying getting louder and more childlike as she approached. But it was not a child but an otter that she found at the edge of the tide, its fur hopelessly clogged with diesel oil. She fetched her brother and he killed and buried it, for there was no saving it.

Jura (7, 19) is so intensely different from Islay that it is a little surprising to see it lying so close across the narrows. It is not a green island at all but dark with moorland. Its appearance is uncompromisingly Highland. Compared with Islay it is a barren place, today with hardly three hundred of a population, about a twentieth of that of Islay. Nor can it ever have been very thickly populated, although, of course, it has suffered the steady draining away of its people along with the rest of the isles. The main centre is along the south-east shore, where there is a wide bay enfolding the four Small Isles. Here there was a good distillery, but it has been disused for many years. Like Lochindaal, Jura's Loch Tarbert almost separates North Jura from South Jura. The hills in the north are not so high as those to the south, conditions generally are kindlier and the present owner is actively improving the sheep-stock. To the south, in Jura Forest, there are hardly any sheep, and the great mountainous wastes are left almost entirely to the deer.

Hardy climbers make a point of climbing all three Paps in a day. I once climbed one, but it was a lovely and entirely satisfying experience. It was a brilliant, hot morning when I crossed by the ferry from Port Askaig. I came ashore by the stalker's cottage at Whitefarland Bay. The deer were grazing peacefully beside his house, but the stalker remarked that they wouldn't be anywhere near when they were wanted. I walked through a wood of dwarfish trees, oak, birch, and holly, through which runs the Glen Asdale Water, making for the nearest Pap, Beinn a'Chaolais. The trees gave out and the Glen Asdale Water sank into a deep gully from which startled deer leapt out, startling me. A hen buzzard rose from a scrubby oak in the gully, soaring above me while I peered down at its two large, ugly, fluffy chicks on their flat platform of twigs. I saw two birds I could not identify, but that I now know to have been Arctic skuas on their most southerly breeding-ground. Gradually the ascent grew steeper, until the "angle of repose" was acute, scree with patches of heather and moss and, all the way to the summit, clumps of sea-pinks.

It was a lovely day, everywhere a golden haze of heat, so that one seemed to travel in a glory. Only at the very top was there a breeze, and there it was quite stiff, making me grateful that the nipple cairn was built like a stone nest wherein one could crouch and look down on the dark gold wastes below. On a clear day the spire of Glasgow Cathedral is said to be visible from the Paps. But today I could only see the sea around in patches through the soft haze, almost 2,500 feet below. It made a wonderful mysterious solitude, a fitting achievement to the long breathless climb. Suddenly an eagle's tail-feather blew towards me on the Pap's crest. I leapt up to catch it. But an eddy of wind caught it, swept it up, out of my reach, and carried it away down into space. The eagle I never saw, but found only the remains of a hare, with a breast-feather beside it.

From Beinn a'Chaolais the sister Paps rise impressively, vastly sloping mountains, with scree-faces, but well formed. There are little lochs at various levels, the broken bits of mirror that mountains drop around them for their reflections. To the

7 Primitive Shielings on Jura, with the Paps behind

8 Oronsay Priory: the Cloisters

Both from engravings after Moses Griffiths in Thomas Pennant's
Tour in Scotland and Voyage to the Hebrides (1772)

9 The fine tombstones of the Maclean chiefs on the Island of Inchkenneth

10 Slate Quarriers' tombstones on the Island of Luing

11 Islay: Port Askaig, looking across the Sound to the Paps of Jura

Oronsay: Carved
head of a Celtic
Cross

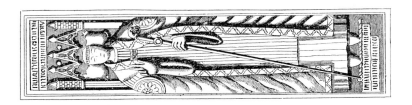

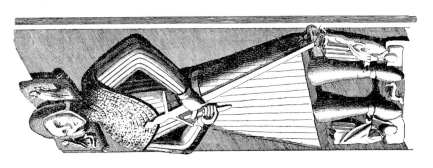

13–17 Slab Tombs in Oronsay

east I could just distinguish through the haze the curious long
arm of land that forms the Lowlandman's Bay and the promontory bounding Loch na Bile wherein are gathered the Small Isles.
I came down by the sheerer slope to the south-east, sometimes
glissading, but the big boulders were inclined to glissade without
my intending it. On a green patch below about sixty head of deer
were grazing or cooling themselves off in the lochans. They barked
and grunted as I came amongst them, and sprang up on all the
promontories around me. I drank from their drinking-place, a cool,
welling spring.

Thereafter followed one of those long, rather wearying wet-
moorland walks, I was glad to be sockless and wearing crepe-
soled sandals which, besides affording an excellent prehensile
grip for climbing, prevent one's feet from becoming waterlogged
when crossing interminable bogs. Forbye, I had only a shirt and
trousers, and gladly took them all off and threw myself into the
Glen Iubharnadale Water—sweet with peat, soft and cool, where
it flowed through a patch of scrub towards the shore. There is a
shore road along the Sound, but a curious one, for every now and
then it drops down to sea level and disappears in pebble beaches
where its continuation is only officially confirmed by the imper-
turbable telegraph poles.

The steamer calls at Jura on its run to and from Port Askaig:
in one day, and out the next. Islay, of course, besides its daily
steamer, has a twice daily, in summer thrice daily, air service.
This puts it within very easy reach of Glasgow, and makes it
the more surprising to find Gaelic so universally spoken amongst
the native people. Islay, indeed, has a considerable tradition of
Gaelic scholarship, for both Neil MacAlpine, the compiler of the
Gaelic dictionary, and John F. Campbell, the folklorist, were
Islaymen, as was also the poet, William Livingstone.

To east and west of Islay and Jura are pairs of islands: Gigha
and Cara to the east, Colonsay and Oronsay to the west. Gigha
is a low-lying island of woods and small farms, visited by the
steamer alternately at the south end, where there is a pier, and
at the north, where a ferryboat meets it. Cara is now uninhabited,

unless by the Brownie, the familiar of the family of MacDonald of Largie; but it too has the remains of a little church. Both lie close in to Kintyre.

Colonsay and Oronsay form a larger group, beyond them the open Atlantic. The name Oronsay is frequently said to derive from St. Oran, one of St. Columba's companions. In fact it is simply a Viking name implying a tidal island, to be found in sometimes slightly varying forms in several places in the Hebrides.

It is most pleasant to land from a small boat on Oronsay, white sand covered with green turf rising gently out of the sea. Outcrops of rock and more green turf carry the land up higher. It is very beautiful on a fair day, very Hebridean, yet with the uniqueness that marks most of the Isles. Over the white sand the sea is that wonderful lucid Iona green, with purple patches over weed and rock. Indeed, it has something of the hallowedness of Iona, for the ruins of the old Priory are still substantial enough to carry meaning (8). Moreover, it is said that Columba landed on Oronsay on his outgait from Ireland, climbed the rise in the centre of the island, and, finding he could still see the Irish coast, pursued his way to his fruitful exile in Iona. It is probable enough that Oronsay was later the home of Celtic monks before becoming a priory of the Augustinian Canons of Holyrood.

The Priory was, of course, flourishing when Sir Donald Munro, High Dean of the Isles, visited it in 1549. Thereafter its history is unrecorded for about a hundred and fifty years, till Martin Martin made his tour. From Martin's account the fabric seems to have been intact in his day, unused, so that the altar remained—as it does to this day—one of the very few mediæval altars left in Scotland. He records that there had been a "modern" crucifix on it, set with precious stones, of which the most valuable was preserved "as a catholicon for diseases". Martin mentions two broken crosses, each about twelve feet in height, besides the splendid high cross, "of an entire stone very hard", that still stands at the west end of the church, a beautiful stone with its crucifix and Celtic patterning of leaves and tendrils and petals. By the time Thomas Pennant reached Oronsay in 1772 the buildings were roofless and one side of the cloisters was down.

Since then there has been further decay of the domestic buildings and another range of the cloisters is away. Although one side of these cloisters is arcaded in a normal way, the other three were unique, at least in Western Europe, being formed of thin stone slabs (which look as though they might have been borrowed from an earlier monastic structure, even perhaps tombstones); these are topped with a plinth supporting two other stones meeting at an acute angle, looking rather like a row of little sentry-boxes. Their small scale and original design are curiously attractive (8).

Now the decay of the Priory buildings has been arrested by the Office of Works, and they stand a ruin substantial enough to be very pleasant. Iona apart, perhaps there is no place in all the Isles that more clearly demands rehabilitation and the return of a religious community able to put to true purpose the intense Hebridean loneliness, softened by the beauty of the green and purple sea and the bright turf and dark rocks; made various by the changing lights.

Now preserved in a re-roofed, once double-storeyed, building are some very fine grave slabs carved in high relief with figures of warriors and priests (13–17). On some, galleys and hunting scenes, swords and flowers and cats stand out against the dark stone. Near the east end of the church a second, smaller cross has been re-erected. It is of Celtic style, unpierced, bearing a beautiful figure of the Christ holding host and chalice.

Some lovely things have come to light in Oronsay, but there is reason to believe that there are more still concealed in the darkness of the earth. There must have been some good people in that priory whose very records are lost.

A little road leads from behind the Priory to the ford that can be crossed at low tide. The Strand, from which the sea entirely recedes, is about a mile across, wet, puddled, patterned with wave-marks. The sand here is not the white shell-sand but rather muddy, of an ochreous colour. On the Colonsay side there is a stretch of saltings thick with short-stemmed sea-pinks and above it the road leads through low hills, forming almost a shallow gully, the sea quite hidden. The hills are rocky, with much heather and bracken, and, where there are some small fields, clumps of bluebells and yellow flags in the wet places. Thereafter the road ahead ascends a steep slope dramatically and disappears through a cutting at the crest. But before that there is a turning to the right that leads to the pleasant, kindly hotel and the pier at Scalasaig. Over the crest the scene changes. One looks down upon a comparatively fertile and cultivated strath, though still rather shut in, with little rocky mountains closing the view at the far end. Beyond these are bird cliffs, and to the west a bold bay of golden sand. The strath is made the brighter by the light reflected from lochs, beyond them trees and the policies of the mansion-house. Here grow many exotic varieties of rhododendrons, delicately trumpeted, of many shades of red, and scented azaleas. In the high-walled garden there are palm trees amongst the currant bushes and cabbages.

II

Jura ends dramatically, its northern tip forming the southern shore of the Corrievreckan Straits. Here a west wind and a flood tide can make a thirty-foot high whirlpool. The Corrievreckan is named after the corrie—a pothole or boiler—on the far side from Jura, and the vreckan, a tartan-patterned rock on the Jura shore. Sometimes, in a calm, there is no trace of the whirlpool to be seen, although there is always a fair tide race through the narrows at the rise and fall.

It is the island of Scarba that lies across the straits, a solid, rather circular island, about three miles across, rising from the sea in a fairly steady slope to almost 1,500 feet. Today a keeper lives in the one inhabited house, though there are one or two other houses still habitable, besides the ruins of a church of more faithful days. Besides red deer, there are the survivors of a herd of fallow, surprising to see. There is fine rough cliff scenery along the coast, and the whole island has a rough and rugged appearance, dark with

18 Gribune Head, Mull

19 Jura, showing one of the Paps

Both from aquatints by William Daniell (1817)

20 Easdale and the slate quarries of Seil, from the air

heather and bracken, although with some clump of trees. Not long ago, on two separate occasions, lobster-fishermen sailing round Scarba had their boats pursued by a whale. Probably it had no intention of attacking, was simply playing, but a forty-foot whale is not a comfortable playmate for the crew of a twenty-foot boat, especially along a coast so rocky as that of Scarba, with hardly a safe landing-place at all.

Immediately north of Scarba is Lunga, uninhabited now, though there is an apparently good house on it. Lunga is used for grazing for Highland cattle by a farmer on Luing. It is smaller and lower and less wild than its neighbour, but a distinctly attractive place with an interestingly indented coastline and a string of small satellite isles to the north. West again lie Eilean Dubh Mor and Eilean Dubh Beag, the Big Black Island and the Little Black Island, and beyond them the Garvellochs or Isles of the Sea. The mother of St. Columba is said to be buried on one of the Garvellochs, although according to some the theory is the invention of kindly Iona boatmen who wished their passengers to feel that they were getting their money's worth. There are, however, some remains of a Celtic monastic settlement to be seen. The sea hereabouts is dangerous with small islands, reefs, and sharp-toothed rocks, on which many ships have been wrecked. Most notable is the little island of Belnahua. This island is composed entirely of slate. For long it was quarried, scooped out well below sea level. The neat little cottages of the quarriers remain, but they are deserted. For the time came when it was considered unsafe to take away any more of Belnahua, lest the island be so weakened that the seas crush it.

Seil (20) and Luing and Easdale remain the slate-quarrying islands. But today hardly any slate is being quarried there at all. The current British policy of "Cheaper and Nastier" (which often proves not to be cheaper, but is always triumphantly nastier) has prevailed. It is now possible to produce exquisitely ugly roofing materials in factories. Craftsmanship is superseded. Automatons can clock in to do the job. The twin octopi, Industrialism and Trade Unionism, have spread their empire. Insult to injury, the impoverished and unemployed people of Seil have now complete synthetic houses to live in, or at least to look at, imported at great cost. Steadings in Luing have been re-roofed with impervious white asbestos sheets, factory-made. The cost of putting up the prefabricated and "non-traditional" houses has of course, in practice, proved far greater than would have been, under any reasonable basis, the building of honest-to-God houses. But it has been a great success in impoverishing such places as Seil and Luing, driving the people into unemployment from which they can be winkled out and exported to the conformity of the industrial areas.

Seil and Luing are sizable islands, lying close in to the mainland. Seil, in fact, may be reached very tamely by road. A fine old bridge, of a single steep span, crosses the Atlantic where it is only the width of a burn, carrying the road from Oban on to the island of Seil. In summer this bridge is a brilliant purple, the south side being overgrown with a flowering Italian alpine plant that flourishes in the mild climate, and is no doubt protected from frosts by the sea air. Thereafter one might expect Seil to be a tame place altogether, but in fact it has some dramatic cliff scenery. On a summer evening I lay on the top of the cliffs overlooking Eilean nan Caorach, watching an eagle winging down from the north. Three of the raven populace of Seil flew out to intercept it. After a few aerobatics they flew off, while the eagle soared contentedly a little off the shore. It swung in again and two of the ravens came out to the attack. The eagle stooped on the foremost raven and it broke flight and fluttered down, cawing. There was then an amusing altercation between the ravens, the hen bird plainly pressing her mate to continue the attack. Eventually his reluctance prevailed, they flew inland, miscalling one another, leaving the eagle to delight me, circling and gently swooping over the long shadows of the cliffs and the silken smooth sea.

Besides its cliffs, Seil has a delightful village, built partly on the small adjacent island of Easdale. Neat white cottages, roofed with the dark island slate, stand in rows in a setting made more watery by a large flooded quarry, on one side the sea and distant islands, on the other a great dark cliff of slate. A jetty and dykes are built of slates up-ended, carrying on the geological formation of the rock. Nearby is a house with a large walled garden filled with flowering shrubs, with clematis spreading profusely over the walls. There are steep green slopes leading to the cliffs and afford-ing beautiful views over the little homesteads to the islanded sea.

Luing is reached from Seil by ferry over the swift water of Cuan Sound. On the Luing Side is a little private quarry from which slates are being cut for roofing the restored Abbey buildings of Iona. The slates are rough, of a pleasing texture, and set with gleaming golden crystals of iron pyrites. These crystals gradually weather away, leaving little angular rusted pits. Fragments of slate lying around Iona Cathedral had these pit-marks, revealing that the original slates had come from quarries in Luing or Seil.

Luing (the *u* is not pronounced—just, as it were, remembered) has two small villages: Cullipool, in the north, where at the time of writing there is still one small quarry working, and Tobero-nochy, to the south, which is far on the road to dereliction. Toberonochy is an attractive place, too, with its neat slated cottages amongst the trees, and its view across a narrow sound to the green isle of Shuna; but some houses are already ruinous and others empty and falling away, and the neighbouring quarry is full of water. Inland from Toberonochy stand the ruins of the pre-Reformation church of Kilchattan in a graveyard full of interest-ing stones. The most remarkable is one, or rather a whole series of slabs of slate, prepared for himself with an enormously long epitaph by one Alexander Campbell of Achadnadure who died in 1829 at the age of seventy-eight. Probably he began his inscription prematurely and, persistently surviving, kept thinking of bits to add to it, Presbyterian propaganda, Biblical quotations, maledictions upon any who might disturb his rest, and strong words on Erastianism. So much, indeed, that the epitaph has split over the churchyard wall and one stone is set so that the passer-by may read it from the road. Slate headstones record the passing of quarriers, one or two of them embellished with quaint cuts of trumpeting angels or Death armed with a spear. A "Late Merchant in Glasgow" has come home to Luing to lie beneath a sandstone slab engraved in graceful copperplate, like the merchant's business card. Two modern stones are of exotic design. They came from Latvia for the graves of Latvian seamen drowned when the *Helena Faulbaums* went down on Belnahua on a stormy October night in 1936. The larger, of granite carved with a sailing ship and a cross, stands over the common grave of fourteen of the crew. The epitaph concludes with the request "Pray for them", which would have seemed the blackest heresy to Alexander Campbell of Achadnadure, but quite natural to the builders of the ruined church. The smaller stone bears a photograph portrait of the wireless operator, and an inscription in broken English: "Radiote Legrath Albert Sultcs. Died Oct. 26th, 1936. Was storm, . . . tore blossoms, Destroyed dreams of happyness. Vegaki, Parents in Latvia."

Over from Kilchattan, on the west shore, is Black Mill Bay, where those who wish to visit neighbouring islands will find an excellent boatman and guide.

The island of Kerrera lies five miles north of Seil, enclosing Oban Bay. While Oban looks better seen from Kerrera, whence the abuse of its superb site by ugly building is not so apparent, Kerrera is in actuality more attractive than it looks. From Oban it looks a bit bald, green, with some overflow of urban shanty building. Beyond this rude introduction there is an amusing, knobbly countryside. On the east coast a bay is filled with sunken craft, boats bored with holes and moored in the sea, a depot for lobsters caught over a wide area. Here the crustaceans are kept alive between creel and cooking. To the south the green land tumbles seaward and, with a last bounce, provides a site for Gylen Castle (21). Gylen is grandly situated: one sees it from the boat on the sail to Iona, standing elegant, wistful in ruin. It is a really nice little tower, built to the L plan, and although pretty ruinous easily restored in the mind's eye. The stair tower is carried up for an extra storey and gabled to provide an extra chamber, access gained by a wee stair corbelled out. The masonry is good, with well-cut mouldings. It fairly fills its knurr of rock and is

21 The coast of Kerrera with Gylen Castle, looking across the
Firth of Lorne to Mull

22 Staffin Bay in Trotternish, Skye

23 Galmisdale below the Sgurr of Eigg

24 Clanranald Pier, Isle of Eigg

25 The Burg Headland, Isle of Mull

26 Skye: cliffs to the north of Portree, Rudha Na Airde Glaise

27 The old Castle of the Macleans of Coll

28 The Parish Church, Lismore, incorporating part of the fabric of the pre-Reformation Cathedral

approached by a built-up bridgeway. Its natural defence is excellent; but it was probably difficult to relieve, as the unfortunate Episcopalian garrison found. They surrendered to the Covenanters on promise of quarter, and many of them were promptly put to death.

Another five miles up the Firth of Lorne, right in the mouth of Loch Linnhe, lies Lismore. It, too, is a green isle, but different from any. A long green isle, almost without defined hills, but rough, with always outcrops of rock, a ubiquitous limestone, the whole isle being a rock of about a dozen miles long and little over a mile wide. The soil is very thin, grey, but sprouts fine crops, and there is good stock everywhere, fat cattle and fat sheep. Attractive croft houses are scattered abroad, mostly very small, single-storey, even occasionally with only one lum, but fairly spruce, almost all white.

Yet the chief feature of Lismore is its setting. It lies in the mouth of the Great Glen, that huge geological fault whose other end opens into the Moray Firth. This low-lying, fertile island is bounded on three sides by the grandest mountain scenery, and on the fourth by the mountains of Mull and the islanded sea with Scarba's mass and the Paps of Jura blue in the distance. On a fine summer day everything gleams and shines and rejoices on Lismore, splashed with the colours of wildflowers, and above it all, beyond the blue water, the mountains rise in peak and range with a kind of affectionate grandeur, standing back, proudly solicitous, not interfering. It is a splendid effect devised by Nature.

Not inappropriately, Lismore is strongly associated with the history of the Highlands and Islands. The Book of the Dean of Lismore is a unique collection, made before the year 1550, of Gaelic poetry, now in the National Library. It was compiled by Sir James MacGregor and is written not in Irish script but in Roman, not with the complicated spelling so alarming to the outsider, but phonetically. It contains poems composed over a long period, including Fenian tales, with that most remarkable dialogue between St. Patrick and Ossian in which the pagan poet makes so moving a defence of the old world of heroic nature against the terrifying force of the greater heroism upheld by the Saint.

Lismore was converted by St. Moluag, who was a contemporary, but being of the Pictish association rather a rival than a colleague of St. Columba. It became the site of the Cathedral Church after the year 1200 when the diocese of Argyll was separated from that of Dunkeld. A few mute faces and scraps of moulding still show in the dullish little church that occupies part of the old site, and founds show in the grass outside the present churchyard (28). From 1801 for about thirty years there was a Catholic seminary on Lismore, the buildings being now incorporated in a later house.

Lying seaward on either side of the church is a ruin. To the south-east, on a rise looking out to Eilean Dubh in the Lynn of Lorne and beyond to the island of Eriska and beyond again to the distant height of Cruachan, is Tirefoor. It is called a castle but is in reality the remains of a broch, that ancient indecipherable form of bield. To the north-west, above the wider waters of the Lynn of Morven, is Castle Coeffin, a vast meaningless wreck of broken tusks of masonry, but, again, beautifully situated, a little bay about the base of its knowe. Coeffin is reputed to have been a Viking stronghold, dating from the long days of Viking sway in the Isles. Legend has it that it was the home of a beautiful princess, Beothail, whose lover died in Norway and who died for love herself and was buried in Lismore. An old Gaelic poem is reputed to have been the plea made by her unquiet spirit to her father and brother to take her remains to her lover's side in Norway. A few lines from it, with the translation as given by Dr. Carmichael in his book *Lismore in Alba*, may be given:

> "Mo thaobh fotham, m'fheoil a lobhadh
> Anns an uir, anns an uir.
> Fiollan fiadhaich, 'n sior iarraidh
> Triomh mo ghlun, triomh mo ghlun.
> . . . Mo chridhe 'cnamh air chul na cloiche
> Sios gu smur, sios gu smur."

In English:

> "My side underneath, the flesh rotting
> In the mould, in the mould.
> The wild centipede, ever searching
> Through my knee, through my knee.
> . . . My heart grinding behind the stone
> Down to dross, down to dross."

Lismore was for long thickly wooded, with many oak trees, but, being virtually without peat, and the inhabitants receiving permission to cut down the trees for fuel, it was quite denuded during the course of the eighteenth century. Even today, though, there are a few well-grown trees to be seen.

Although the crofts are good and ample, averaging around forty acres, and despite easy access to Oban and the mainland, Lismore has suffered the same draining away of its population as the other islands. A century and a half ago there were 900 people on Lismore. Today there are barely 200, and the school population is unusually low in proportion, about twenty.

III

Skye apart, Mull is the largest of the Inner Hebrides (25). It is a great tattered island, of such diversity as to seem a miniature country, Highland and Lowland, woodland and farmland, moorland and seaboard. Generally, the landscapes are fairly similar to the southern Highland countrysides of mainland Argyll and Perthshire, only the sea is seldom long out of sight.

The least indented coast is the strip to the north-east, along the Sound of Mull, where most of the much-dwindled population lives today. Lying at the northern end of the Sound, Tobermory, "The Well of Mary", is the main township (29). It stands round a bay that, protected by a small island, provides the best harbourage along the coast. Tobermory was developed as a fishing port by the Scottish Fishery Board towards the end of the eighteenth century, not very successfully; but it retains along the harbourside a good many pleasant houses of the period, gabled and painted white or ox-blood red, or black and white, neatly looking on the sea. Above them is sheer rock or rock tree-clad, and some scrambling houses, then a higher level of pleasant homely Scots houses. The last thatched cottages, many of them once the homes of unfortunate evicted crofters, have gone. The new houses on the inland out-skirts of Tobermory are more happily grouped than is common, helped by varied slopes. Tobermory has long been renowned for the Spanish Armada treasure that, it is confidently hoped, may lie in its bay and of which many stories are told.

From Tobermory a high, switchbacking, twisting, exhilarating road leads west by the Mishnish Lochs to Dervaig, which has one of the most attractive and architecturally unspoilt little hotels in Scotland, harled and yellow-colourwashed with sulphate of copper. Beyond Dervaig the road is more level, leading by the sands of Calgary Bay, then south again before bearing east by Loch Tuath whose waters narrow to an island-broken channel where the Ulva ferry crosses.

Never have I seen desolation less abominable: but desolation it is, Ulva. The island has had an unhappy history, and for the last hundred years has had hardly any history, for the new laird of a century ago cleared the native people from the land to make room for sheep. Within about thirty years he reduced the popula-tion from 360 to 51. Today there is only a handful of people, and very few sheep either. The whole island is stricken with a rank growth of bracken. When there were men to till and cattle to graze, the bracken had no chance to spread. But sheep by themselves are no enemy to bracken. Over Ulva has fallen the Nemesis of the grasping laird. Almost the whole of it is a wilderness of bracken, with everywhere the larochs of well-built little cottages, falling away, tumbled tombstones to a vanished race. A notable race they were too, and left their mark far across the world. David Livingstone's parents came penniless from Ulva to the black, sweated industrialism of Blantyre. Besides Africa, Australia was largely explored by an Ulva man, General MacQuarrie, son of a small farmer, who became Governor of New South Wales and carried out indefatigable explorations before returning to Mull, where he died in 1824 at the age of one hundred and three.

29 The Harbour at Tobermory in Mull

30 The Harbour at Portree in Skye

The north shore of Ulva is somewhat bald, but it faces an attractive arm of the sea, so blue on a good day that it seems unnatural to see a great pure white waterfall pour into it over on the Mull side. Before the new bracken has turned umbelliferous, Ulva is bright with primroses, bluebells, celandines, wild strawberry. It has some trees, and some lovely wooded gullies containing burns running south, where, along the shore, are abrupt clumps of columnar rock. Here lie little isles, the loveliest the sandy, shapely island of Inchkenneth, scooped up from the sea, a long petrified wave. Here in 1773 Johnson and Boswell spent "the 19th Sunday after Trinity. I shall ever remember it. Mr. Johnson said it was the most agreeable Sunday evening he had ever spent in his life. We were all in a good frame. I was truly pious." It is very understandable: Inchkenneth has the quality of a holy place, in its solitude and the remains of its little church, where Boswell reinterred the bones that he found lying scattered. Johnson approved of this act of piety, which he confessed he could not have done himself because of "his horror at dead men's bones". But both travellers were highly delighted by their host, the soldierly Sir Allan Maclean, and his two charming daughters. And both romanced happily, as so many of us have done, of how they might settle forever on this Hebridean island. There was only one drawback:

"It is a kind of objection to Inchkenneth that sometimes the sea between it and Mull is at one place so shallow that people may wade over. This breaks the natural seclusion of being surrounded by the sea. But it is a very rare thing to have so shallow a sea; and even then there are none can pass but people particularly well-acquainted with the place, as there are quicksands. I can have a battery of cannon on that quarter."

West of Ulva, and linked to it by a bridge, is low-lying, fertile Gometra; east again, right within the waters of Loch na Keal, the high little moorland lump of Eorsa.

High above looms the mighty curved crest of Ben More, highest of the Hebridean mountains outside the Cuillin, familiar from afar to all airts, a fantastic viewpoint on a clear day. There is a good breathless ascent up the southern shoulder, with a breakneck descent down a huge scree face to the south-east. From the summit

4*

of Ben More one looks down upon a fantastic world of broken
barrenness: there is a lower, eastern top, but a pitiless drop separates the main summit from the ridge leading to it. All around there
are sheer or near sheer drops: such space about one that one begins
to feel the ample crest itself precarious. Far into the summer small
patches of deep snow gleam in rifts. Coming down to the east
there is a track through Glen Clachaig, dramatic and attractive
seen from the height, with a funeral cairn at the top of the pass;
but a wearisome walk, not worst the bits merely rubbed out by
landslides, but merciless those adopted as convenient beds by
incessant burns. It opens out on to the watery stretch of Loch
Ba.

North-east from Loch Ba, again on the sheltered customarily
tranquil waters of the Sound of Mull, lies Salen, a pleasing enough
small township save for the pre-fabs and "non-traditional"
excrescences that now blot its outskirts. It is a sorry business to
see Mull loaded with this trash of industrialism. The Industrial-
ists, Capital and Labour, with witless spite against sanity and
decency, at last, after 1945, got some control over the building
industry, which hitherto had made some satisfactory demand upon
craftsmanship. They persuaded a willing posse of politicians to
allow them to foist upon the country a wonderful selection of
deformed "building": stuff made of all kinds of unsuitable
materials: porous materials that let the water in from without;
impervious materials that condense it successfully from within;
materials that crack and break. All with only two things in
common, ugliness and the facility to be manufactured by factory-
hands bribed to joylessness by high wages and the despairing
hope of winning freedom through the football pools. As a far-flung
gesture of venom, this excrement of a barren civilisation is per-
petrated, in the shape of a single boot-box pre-fab, right at the
end of the Ross of Mull overlooking the ferry to the Holy Isle of
Iona, as though ready to spring across if given half an official
word of encouragement.

Within sight of this outpost of neo-barbarism on the Ross of
Mull there is a quarry of beautiful pink granite, now unused,

with the quarriers' houses at Bunessan empty and falling away. All around, the rock is granitic, unusual in being set on the perpendicular reed—or grain. Besides the pink stone, some is grey, weathering to a rusty colour. The Mull granite has built some noble things, from the Cathedral and Abbey of Iona to the splendid lighthouses of Skerryvore and Dhuheartach. Huge stones were taken to London for the piers of Blackfriars Bridge. It was given the doubtful honour of being used for the Albert Memorial, but is not to be judged by its use, or rather misuse, there: for granite is by nature a rough, granular stone, and should never be given a shiny marble surface, polished until it looks like a prefabricated galantine fresh from the tin. I have heard an Aberdeen granite master, who tried to get permission to reopen the quarry at Fionphort, say that it is a better stone than that of Peterhead, besides being extremely accessible, easily transported by sea from the pier opposite Eilean nam Ban.

Only the most shameless cooking of books, by which industrial processes are made to appear "more economical" and anything else "not a commercial proposition", could have deceived anyone that it was cheaper to import the manufactured article instead of using the material lying to hand. In fact, of course, it proved ruinously expensive and the cost of the trash that has replaced our houses and homes and defiled our countryside is something that nobody dares to disclose.

The Ross of Mull is a long index pointing from the south of Mull to Iona. The road runs back along Loch Scridain into the heart of the hill-country, coming out into woods, and many cut woods, above Loch Spelve. Ahead lies Grass Point, nearest to Oban, with a pleasant white house, recently restored, once an inn for drovers bringing their beasts to the mainland. The next promontory to the north is Duart Point, with the imposing castle of the Macleans a familiar and cherished landmark. The Macleans of Duart, with their various cadet families, Maclaines of Lochbuie (who, incidentally, claimed priority), Macleans of Brolas, Aros, Pennycross, and Torloisk, and of Coll, for long held sway, often a pretty bloody sway, over Mull and its neighbouring islands.

Their power was ultimately broken in 1691 when Sir John Maclean surrendered to Argyll. Nearly a hundred years later, when he stayed on Inchkenneth with Sir Allan Maclean, Boswell was hoping that they might yet be successful in reclaiming their lands. At last the late Sir Fitzroy Maclean bought back Duart and its Point. The Castle, which had been used as a military garrison and left to become ruinous, was restored in 1912. It was done, on the whole, with excellent judgment, and stands to delight those who travel through the Sound of Mull, high on its rock above the shore, set against the mountains. The purist might quibble at a large window opened in the seaward wall, but its effect from within, framing an incomparable view over the sea and up mountain-enchasmed Loch Linnhe, is its justification.

Beyond Duart and the contrasting Victorian baronialism of Torosay Castle, lies Craignure, with its neat little inn and small pier serving the ferry that meets the steamer from Oban. From here the road winds along the coast to Salen by little bays where eider duck and divers swim, with one strikingly fine piece of scenery, the view up Glen Forsa to the shapely double peak of Ben Talla.

The dispossession of its crofters robbed Mull of much of its native population. Comparatively little Gaelic is spoken there today. Many of the people are incomers or the descendants of incomers. I asked an Aberdeen forester how he liked living in Mull. "I've been here four years," he said appreciatively, "and I'd never have had so many laughs on the mainland." In the great days of Highland sporting estates much of the land was bought by people from the south. The incursus, from Scotland and from England, is slower now, but more wholesome for the island. Those coming now tend rather to come to stay, redeeming the neglected farmland, reviving Mull. Not that they have as yet stemmed the decline, but they bring hope. Highlanders, and *soi-distant* Highlanders living in Glasgow and other distant places (and Glasgow, however near by crowflight, is a million metaphorical miles from the Isles), are sometimes scornful of incoming settlers. But it is folly to be sentimental about blood and the Gaelic tongue. Desirable though it might be to see the Islesmen reclaim their heritage by themselves, there are too few of them now, too impoverished, and too deeved by the incessant propaganda of Industrialism growing shriller as it approaches its nemesis. Any person of good will who will bring infectious life back to the Isles is more important to them than any of those who sigh for them from afar, or even those who set up committees to wring justice from a Government congenitally hostile to a peasant people.

Mull, for its size and interest, has been comparatively little written about. The same cannot be said of Iona, which must comprise three of the most publicised square miles in any remote place : often rather lushly described by writers whose genuine enthusiasm is not matched by talents equally developed. Nor have all the artists who have felt the inspiration of Iona's colouring been able to convey it felicitously on canvas or sketch-block. The result is that a first visit to Iona is commonly made with deep misgiving.

In summer Iona can be reached direct by steamer from Oban. Otherwise the approach is made by way of the Mull steamer, the *Lochinvar*, that puffs up the Sound every weekday while its passengers enthuse over the scenery or shelter from the rain and take their refreshment in a saloon delectably garnished with pictures of the intrepid Young Lochinvar. Descending from the steamer into the ferry at Craignure, the journey to Iona continues by way of a bus through narrow Glen More, once marked with monoliths for the guidance of pilgrims, romantic in sunshine or peculiarly bleak in rain. The world opens out again as the bus runs along the shore road by Loch Scridain, through the Ross of Mull to Fionphort and the Iona ferry. The sea voyage is made along the south of Mull, round the Ross between pretty bays and horrid rocks, into the Sound of Iona.

It is possible that the visitor who saw Iona only in the worst Hebridean weather might retain a distaste for it: otherwise only the ingrained, phrenetick, sentimentally cynical, could maintain his misgiving in face of the reality. Iona is a place of amazing beauty. A simplicitude of beauty, and a beatitude: for it is difficult to dismiss that sense as of a place hallowed, the atmosphere left marked with the impress of the presence of holy people. It is a feeling hard to fix, hard to be sure of, yet potent: the occasion of Dr. Johnson's famous: "That man is little to be envied, whose patriotism would not gain force upon the plain of *Marathon*, or whose piety would not grow warmer among the ruins of *Iona*." Boswell, with his brilliant candour, declared that as he knelt in Iona Cathedral he "hoped that ever after having been in this holy place, I should maintain an exemplary conduct". Right and admirable, but of course the sense cannot be capitalised: Boswell, and we, fall from grace again with painful celerity. Whatever it is, the Iona atmosphere remains too insubstantial of itself to rebuild ourselves upon. Yet that does not discountenance the reality of the atmosphere, only, perhaps, the integrity of our motives; we want, as too often, to carry something tangible away with us, being insufficient in the instantaneous joy of experience that, in fact, can alone give us something to take away, but it is something hardly even of memory, certainly unmarketable.

It is easier to try to analyse the physical beauty of Iona. Much lies in the colouring, stretches of immaculate white sand shelving into the water and there turning Iona green, sometimes varying into ranges of darker greens or brighter blues: the water over the tangle often fantastically empurpled. The crisp turf is a bright sappy green, the Cathedral walls a warm red. Then there are beaches that are not sandy, one little bay in particular that seems filled with brilliant gems; even upon inspection they retain their brilliance, if not their fancy value: water-worn scraps of the fine green marble, of Mull's pink granite, white chuckies, black stones covered with brilliants. The size and the shape of Iona, too, are beautiful: the size compassable, the shape delicate, wind-turned dunes, the 332-foot eminence of Dun I, Iona's hill, correct in scale. The Cathedral, and the Abbey walls rising again about it, the crosses and the ruins, are beautiful (32): the view beyond, to the mountains of Mull or the little islands lying to the north,

Staffa, the Dutchman's Cap, and the Treshnish Isles, the sun on their southern faces. I must confess that I have never been in Iona in relentless winter rains, only in summer rains, comparatively kindly, drawn across the island like grey veils, always a bright gleam to be seen somewhere, it might be the sand or the sea itself, making the grey evanescent, transient.

Yet doubtless colours and shapes and buildings are not of themselves enough. Perhaps as in the case of a lovely face, beauty of place is at the last beyond analysis, born of integration rather than composed of several elements: and then . . . We hesitate, return to wondering whether perhaps, even as with the face, there is behind the integration itself something of a personality in a place. So, having come full circle while adding one more to the deterrent word-pictures of Iona, I can best recommend the reader to go and assess for himself.

It was in 563 that Columba landed in Iona, exiled from Ireland by his own violent temper. He came to a right place to learn sanctity: from all his hectic excursions he returned to the Iona quiet, the stimulus of its summers, and the chastening of the Hebridean winters. His monastery, composed of separate wood or wattle cells, with "offices" in the shape of barn, byre, mill, and refectory for the common meal, stood, with the chapel (probably all within the usual "cashel", a defensive earthern bank), about a quarter of a mile to the north of the present cathedral. It is assumed that after the Viking invasions of about the year 800 the Columban monastery was rebuilt, in stone, by the present site, where there are some remains of late Irish type, including the stump of a round tower. But the Abbey buildings and the church as we know them and as they are today being reconstructed are Benedictine foundations of the twelfth century.

There is, unfortunately, a lot of nonsense written and talked about the Celtic Church, dating from the late Victorian era when some Scottish divine, less learned than fantastic, tried to present it as a schismatic body. There was, of course, never any question of schism. However reluctant the Culdee monks may have been to give up the one or two minor distinctions that had crept into their practices during long years of isolation, they never dreamt of themselves as being separated from the main body of the Church, and conformed when commanded at the Synod of Whitby. Yet the elaborate myth of all manner of different rites continues to grow with youthful vigour and some ludicrous effects.

The Benedictine Abbey of Iona and the neighbouring priory of Augustinian Canonesses flourished until the Reformation. For a short time, indeed, its church was a cathedral, after the Sodores, or Southern Isles, became a separate docese from the original joint diocese of Sodor and Man. After 1561 the monks and nuns, with their manuscripts and beautiful church ornaments, were scattered: some found their way to monasteries abroad, where manuscript copies of Adamnan's Life of St. Columba that perhaps came out of Iona at that time are still preserved. In 1635 Iona was seized by the Macleans of Duart, and in 1693 it was taken from them by the Argyll family. Throughout this long time the buildings, and the tombs of those Scottish, Irish, Norwegian, and, it was said, even French kings or chieftains who had sought burial on the holy isle, suffered complete neglect. In 1899 the ruins were presented to the Church of Scotland. The Abbey church was restored, on the whole well, immediately afterwards. The conventual buildings are today being reconstructed on the old foundations by the Iona Community of the Rev. Dr. George Macleod. This reconstruction is being carried out with great sensibility by Mr. Ian Lindsay, an architect with a thorough appreciation of Scottish Gothic characteristics. The newly completed refectory, much of it rebuilt almost from ground level, is a splendid massive barrel-vaulted chamber. It is a delight to know that any such thing should be built in an age that has sponsored the barbarian hutments of the pre-fabs.

Concerning the Iona Community itself there is often some confusion. Dr. Macleod has been accused of monasticism, but there is nothing remotely monastic about his community. Throughout the year tradesmen, masons and joiners, live in the huts provided alongside the Abbey buildings, carrying out the work of rebuilding.

32 Iona: the Cathedral, St. Oran's Chapel and the Burial Place of the Kings

22 "Loch Ranza Bay, and the Manner of Taking the Basking Shark."

For two or three months each year Dr. Macleod holds a kind of summer-school on the island for young ministers, who also give some help with the labouring. The precepts of St. Columba, that derived from the monasticism of St. Martin of Tours and were developed into that of St. Benedict, are, as such, still with us, but not in Iona. The atmosphere is there but, as has been remarked, atmosphere is not enough.

The daily summer trip from Oban that calls at Iona makes its next stop at Staffa (2), where the visitors parade to observe the wonders of Fingal's Cave (34). It is a venerable tourist trip. It is consoling to know that, making the visit in 1833, Wordsworth felt as we have felt, and recorded his feeling with greater irritation than poetry:

> "We saw but surely, in that motley crowd,
> Not one of us has felt the far famed sight;
> How *could* we feel it? each the others blight,
> Hurried and hurrying, volatile and loud."

Sir Joseph Banks, the naturalist, is customarily credited with having "discovered" Staffa in the year 1772. There was, to be sure, already a house on the island, and the caves had been given their Gaelic names, Staffa itself its Norse one, but, apart from a passing reference in George Buchanan's *History of Scotland* of 1582, there seems to be no earlier printed description than the account given by Sir Joseph. A pretty constant heavy swell round the steep rocky coastline of Staffa made it, although lying near to Mull, never regularly inhabited, used only for summer grazing. Its "discovery" created a good deal of interest; its colonnades and caves of columnar basalt ringing fashionable echoes in days of gothick enthusiasm, and it was repeatedly declared "an improvement upon the Works of Art". In 1817 William Daniell issued a volume of nine coloured acquatint views of Staffa, not amongst his more accurate delineations—he was perhaps concerned to complete his sketches speedily to get away before the seas became angry again. Shortly afterwards Turner did his painting, and Mendelssohn established Fingal's Cave as a concert piece. Indeed, Staffa is a most imposing geological freak with its columns of basaltic rock squeezed into colonnades and carved into caves, a wild and handsome place, an awesome work of Nature; but it needs surely to be visited at leisure with some peace and solitude properly to taste the desolate, inanimate primæval thrill of it. Out from Staffa stand the Bac Mor, the Dutchman's Cap, but it is like a wide-brimmed beaver, and its little neighbour, the Bac Beag, separate only at high tide. They were once used for summer grazing, for nineteen cattle, it being said that "twenty would starve". North again lie the Treshnish Isles, once with a castle for a small garrison, long desolate, left to the creatures of sea and air. Two large low-lying islands stand out from Mull looking across twenty miles of the Minch to the Outer Isles: Coll and Tiree.

Although it has two low hills to west and south, Ben Hough and Ben Hynish, the main, immediate, and persistent impression given by Tiree is one of a tremendous flatness: on a fine bright day a brilliant green flatness contained beneath a great domed bowl of sky. There is a rare and exhilarating quality to the sense of space and light, often maintained by the winds that sweep unchecked from sea to sea; a cruel north wind, maybe, a saline, tonic wind tearing the skin from one's jowl as one battles along the shelterless machair. It is a terrific quality this of light, light pouring from the sky and bouncing back from the sea, enveloping everything, seeming shadow-free. Wind-spun clouds leap across the bowl of sky from horizon to horizon. Bright sands stretch along wide curved bays. Everything seems fresh painted.

Stevenson had his base at Hynish for the building of the lighthouse of Skerryvore. It makes a great story, the tale of how the remote storm-hashed skerry was ultimately made to support a high bell-cast tower of granite flashing its light for fifty miles. The granite came from Mull and was prepared by Aberdeen masons, dovetailed and joggled so that every stone interlocks and no single stone could be removed without taking down every stone above it. Even the floors are of granite slabs binding wall to wall. There are still a few unused stones left by the lightkeepers' houses at Hynish. The little pier and harbour basin—flooded with the water from the dam built just above to float out the boat loaded with prepared granite—are still there, fresh and clean as though they had been built yesterday instead of a hundred years ago, soft, pink Mull granite. It is all so neat and pleasant that the contrast of the abandoned Official works of the 1940's stands out in horrific contrast. During the '39 war Tiree was a base for thousands of airmen, far outnumbering the native population. Nasty black runways cut across the wonderful impervious green turf of the Reef (the central belt of Tiree). Hutments spread from them in all directions. When I visited Tiree five years after the war was over I found the most appalling and indescribable mess of half-demolished hutments, scattered sheets of rusty iron, broken concrete beds, every kind of squalid waste. Tiree was never bombed, but five years after the war it looked more like a bombed area than any bombed area in Britain. Bombed places had been tidied up: Tiree had been messed up. Officialdom cared nothing for the remote places. Much had been sold for scrap, with no compulsion upon the purchaser to make a clean job when he took what he wanted away. Nobody could tell me when, if ever, the demolition was to be completed. It seemed as though this despoliation was to be left testament to the venom of the modern world, the palpable expression of the nastiness once put upon canvas by the surrealists. Bombs were not needed to create this effect, it was simply part of the same picture; it made the atom bomb so much more understandable, an inevitable apotheosis, nothing extraneous but an ultimate achievement of moral irresponsibility, the last witless, God-forsaking gesture. On the outskirts of an industrial town one might scarcely have remarked on the squalor of these ruins; but it was revealing to see them set against the wide-stretching, sky-reflecting beauty of Tiree.

There is some variety of houses in Tiree (4, 5). A good many are of blackhouse type, but hardly one is still thatched. Chiefly they have curious abrupt roofs covered with tarred felt, often not oversailing the wallhead at all but rising a couple of feet back.

The reason for this is that the blackhouses were generally double-walled, the space between the two being filled with earth or, as at Tiree, with sand. The total wall may be three or four feet thick, and the thatched roofs themselves always terminated on the inside wall. It is thought that this was chiefly because of the shortage of timber which made it desirable to reduce its use as far as possible—such queer twisted bits of driftwood as sometimes serve as beams in blackhouses could not be asked to present any larger area of thatch to the wind than was essential. It is possible too that in days when there were no rhones it was considered a lesser evil that rainwater from the roof should run into the earthern heart of the wall rather than form a quagmire around the house. One quaint effect that the abbreviated roof-pitch gives to the refurbished blackhouses of Tiree is the open-to-the-sky window apertures, which commonly have no lintel and which, being very deep, jag into the otherwise trim bield. Besides being now limed or cemented the jointing of the Tiree houses is sometimes painted with wide white bands leaving only the centres of the stones bare, patterning the house like the hide of a giraffe. A very different building is the factor's house, standing white on an island in a freshwater loch, reached by a causeway, an ampler building altogether; but there are a number of fairly old small farmhouses and the like amongst the homesteads scattered wide over the island.

Tiree has a daily plane service, and is otherwise reached by the Oban boat that sails by Tobermory and Coll and goes on to Lochboisdale, outwards one day and inwards the next, weather permitting. The boat now comes in to a new pier at Gott Bay in the northern part of the island. A little to the south at Scarinish, still the main centre of population, is the old harbourage, the delightful small bay of Scarinish, too small for the large boats but still with small craft and a brief pier, where coal puffers can unload. I came on this bay from the south on a day in 1950, coming down to it suddenly, hardly able to believe my eyes, thinking I saw an inanimate ghost. A large schooner lay gently heeled over on her side, masted and all, seemingly intact, the whole hulk a wonderful

34 Fingal's Cave, Staffa

soft weathered grey, most ghostlike against the bright green, sunlit blue water and the amiable commonplace bright red of a newly painted little puffer tied up at the pier. Coming closer I could see her name in faint gold lettering, *Mary Stewart*. I inquired of a man in white sea boots, who told me simply, "The old man died." It seemed the *Mary Stewart's* old man had died twenty years before and she, almost the last sailing boat to trade about these coasts, had lain there in peaceful, respected decay ever since. "But you'd miss her if she wasn't there," he said. She was a beautiful ship of some seventy tons, built ninety-three years before.

Gott Bay, known as the silversands, is rather bald; the sands within Hynish Bay, especially those of Sorobaidh, are more pleasingly laid out. Some of the north coast is rocky, or pebbly. Balephuill Bay has Iona pebbles, moss agates and clear white "Tiree Crystals", which people gather and have cut and mounted. Tiree, in fact, is closely linked with Iona. St. Baithene, cousin of St. Columba, and one of the twelve who accompanied him from Ireland, was put in charge of the foundation Columba made in Tiree in 563; he later succeeded Columba in Iona. Tiree is identified with Ethica Insula of Adamnan, and Regio Hyth of the Irish chronicles. St. Columbanus was ordained by Columba in Hyth. It contained a great number of chapels: fifteen were counted at the end of the eighteenth century, largely with Irish dedications, although fragments of only a bare half-dozen remain today, with two or three ancient crosses, including St. Michael's Cross at Sorobaidh, a memorial to an abbess of Iona of 1543. Under Protestantism Tiree took an independent course and was for some time a stronghold of the Baptists, who used to immerse their members in Loch an Eilean.

Tiree did not suffer from the earlier Highland depopulation; in fact it seems to have reached its peak about 1881, when there were 2,730 people on the island. Since then it has come down to about 1,200. The crofts are of fifteen to twenty acres, with excellent common grazing on the sandy machair. It breeds big-boned cattle which are sold largely to English buyers.

Coll lies north-east of Tiree with the little isle of Gunna a giant's stepping-stone between. Although so close, and likewise low-lying, it is a perfectly different island. I met a Coll man once and told him I hoped one day to visit Coll, which he had been praising. He became quite nervous, warning me not to be put off by my first sight of his homeland. Certainly a first sight of the east coast is most unprepossessing. It has not got the breath-taking flatness of Tiree but is a slightly elevated monotonous corrugated barrier of wet-looking rock-bespattered moorland above a rocky shore. The only feature as one arrives on the steamer is, if it is summer and one is lucky, the dorsal fins of basking sharks that dearly like this unpromising coast and often weave along it in shoals of about a score, great big black shining, harmless brutes. The only harbourage is in Loch Eotharna, into which on October 3rd, 1773, young Coll brought his boat with Johnson and Boswell on a stormy, frightening night, with Boswell holding tight to a rope attached to the top of a mast, serving no purpose whatever but to keep him quiet, while Johnson lay "in philosophic tranquility, with a greyhound of Coll's at his back keeping him warm".

The only remaining village on Coll lies above the pier at Arinagour, a row of white cottages with oddly high-set windows, nice but marred by corrugated iron hutments and an awful tangle of every kind of rubbish overflowing on to the beach. Round the bay stands the little hotel of a kindliness and hospitality that one will not forget: tumblers of cream, home-made biscuits, and a knowledgeable hostess.

Much of Coll does indeed consist of the soggy rocky moorland that one sees when making the eastern approach, bad walking, wet and laborious, making it better to stick to the roads. But in extreme contrast there is a wonderful sandy machair along the west end and at either end: sand dunes and stretching shores of a fine piled sand that can hardly have an equal the world over. Coming down to the shore beyond Gallanach and the burial ground with its defaced stones to Macleans, there is an enchanting strand, white-gold, of sunlit sand with towering wind-moulded dunes, peacock-green and kingfisher-blue seas, set in little rock-bound bays: wonderful stretches of sand with the tide racing to meet itself again round little islets of rock—a hard, sensible rock of various colours. Along here I saw some seals loitering. I paddled out to an island rock and five seals bobbed up around me, interested. I sang to them, they seemed delighted. I became so convinced of their enthusiasm that I half expected them to clap their flippers. To be truthful they did not, but I still felt I had proved that seals were not truly musical creatures. There is a lot of bird life along these shores: spick, span oyster-catchers wheel and peal, little dunlin, very tame, drive in flocks about one's feet, out to sea mallard and shelduck and wigeon swim, terns uptail and dive, gannets abandon themselves to space. Over their bright bed the waves scintillate. It is a brave and glorious world, a sort of companionate solitude, beasts and birds not breaking it but sharing it. The wind-turned dunes, patterned with tufts of bents and their shadows, look near-white in the sunshine. See them again on a sunless day and they still seem lit up, with an inner glow, a private store of sunshine. I think the cause of this may lie in a trace of pink, so slight as often hardly to colour the sand, derived from a pinkish crystalline rock which shines from many outcrops on Coll. Farther south, beyond Grishipoll and Hogh Bay, are small bays of fine gravel or bold rounded pebbles cunningly layered and graded by the sea. Farther again is the Traig Foill, a sheer stretch of sand. Here I saw a great herd of many-coloured cattle being driven, wandering by the sea's edge, over to Crossapol and Caoles, machair country renowned for its beasts. Foill Bay is one side of a neck of sand-dunes, rising high and interesting, the other being formed by the bolder bay of Crossapol on the east side of the island. Farther east is Loch Breakacha, with two castles.

The old castle of the Macleans, to squeeze through whose narrow passages Dr. Johnson had to open his waistcoat, is still substantial but in the last stages of tottering decay (27). A most attractive place it has been, a tower extended at various periods, with a screen wall later developed into a seventeenth-century range and a round tower curiously vaulted. Here starlings and pigeons sit on their nests, so little disturbed that they wait to rise scarifyingly close to the head of the rare visitor. It stands close down to the sea, behind it its successor, a psuedo-castle of 1750, most rightly stigmatised by Johnson as a tradesman's box. Pity it ever was built and the old homestead left to moither. It is quite astonishingly bad for so early a period, more like an early Victorian villa than an eighteenth-century conceit. It, too, is empty now. The huge walled garden of the period, lying across Loch Breachacha, has been more imposing, but its garden house, ill-sheltered by two windblown palm trees, is spoilt by a clumsy addition.

The ground being more broken, one or two trees have raised their heads in Coll—Tiree is completely treeless. The island is a mixture of machair and the wet moorland that is generally dull but not always unattractive, at its best when the catkins of the bog myrtle are giving place to leaves, the bog bean is in brave flower, and the bog cotton catkins are turning to silverspun cotton. There are two score of freshwater lochs, mostly small but containing trout.

In his day Boswell reckoned the population of Coll at about 1,200. It was higher by the middle of the nineteenth century. The people had a reputation for hard work, and the island was by no means poor. But the Maclean property and the two separate smaller estates at either end of the island fell upon evil days. Maclean, who had a good reputation, could no longer help his people and eventually sold out. By 1901 the population was down to 432. Fifty years later it is hardly half that number. There are only half a dozen crofts; the rest of the land is farmed in fairly substantial units.

It was the young Maclean of Coll whom Dr. Johnson considered the complete islesman:

"He is a noble animal. He is as complete an islander as mortality can figure. He is a farmer, a sailor, a hunter, a fisher; he will run you down a dog. If any man has a tail, it is Coll. He is hospitable; and he has an intrepedity of talk, whether he understands the subject or not."

He appreciated also the old minister of Coll, the Rev. Hector Maclean:

"Mr. Maclean has the reputation of great learning: he is 77 years old, but not infirm, with a look of venerable dignity, excelling what I remember in any other man. His conversation was not unsuitable to his appearance. I lost some of his goodwill, by treating a heretical writer with more regard than, in his opinion, a heretick could deserve. I honoured his orthodoxy, and did not much censure his asperity. A man who has settled his opinions, does not love to have the tranquillity of his conviction disturbed; and at 77 it is time to be in earnest."

IV

The four islands Rhum, Eigg (31), Canna, and Muck together comprise the Parish of the Small Isles. They lie, a self-contained unit between the two substantial lands of Mull and Skye, quite close in to the coast, opposite Mallaig and the celebrated white sands of Morar. Unlike the southern Inner Hebrides, which are all part of Argyllshire, they are considered as part of Inverness-shire (although Canna was for a time credited to Argyllshire). The total population now stands at under 200. Eigg is the home of more than half, and the religious, scientific, administrative, and commercial centre, containing the residences of the priest, minister, doctor, registrar, and the site of the one shop. Three times a week one of the MacBrayne boats, usually the *Loch Mor*, visits the Small Isles. On Monday she calls on her outward journey from Mallaig to the Outer Hebrides, being met by ferry boats at Eigg and Rhum, where there are no piers but only small slipways, and coming in to the tidy little pier at Canna. Passengers and goods for Muck are left at Eigg and called for by private motor launch. On Thursday the calls are made in reverse as the *Loch Mor* sails back to Mallaig. On Saturday there is a round trip from Mallaig which serves also the little pancake of an island, Soay, lying under the lee of the enormous Cuillins, the mountains of Skye. Except perhaps at the height of summer, storm may at any time interrupt the service to one or all of the islands.

On fine summer days there are motorboat trips from Mallaig to Eigg.

Muck—Dean Monro calls it Swynes Ile in literal translation of its Gaelic name—has an adjoining tidal island, Eilean nan Each or Horse Island. The total length is a bare three miles of uneven ground, rising at one point to 450 feet, fairly fertile. There is a sheltered harbour to the south-east, but it is small and has a difficult entry. The laird keeps a good garden and is an active farmer, growing fine crops of potatoes and, true to the island's historic reputation, breeding pigs. There are some nice sandy bays, with a fine view of the three neighbouring islands. On the reefs between Muck and Eigg seals like to bask. There is an old man in Muck who has some very circumstantial accounts of fairies he has seen, and heard piping, and a fairy boat lying in the bay with a little dog in it.

Rhum, lying to the north, is a much larger island although having no larger a population than Muck, a little over a score and none of these native. It has, in fact, never been a very thickly populated island, having little arable land, although its hills provide fine grazing. The story goes that it was part of the Clanranald country, until the MacDonald chieftain traded it to Maclean of Coll for a galley. The galley proved to be rotten, so it was a bad bargain for Clanranald, also for the natives of the island, who were Catholics, for Coll sent his factor over with a yellow stick, before which the people had to bow, renouncing their religion. One of the MacQuarries, part of the Ulva clan who had been dispersed into Coll and Rhum, refused to make obeisance, and Clanranald gave him a holding on Eigg, where his descendants remain. Pennant records a population of 325 in 1772, almost all Protestant but without minister or church, remarking: "The attention of our *popish* ancestors in this article, delivers down a great reproach on the negligence of their reformed descendants: the one leaving not even the most distant and savage part of our dominions without a place of worship; the other suffering the natives to want both instructor, and temple." By the time Hugh Miller visited the island in the *Betsy* it was to record that in 1828, except for one family, the entire population of just over 400 had been shipped across the Atlantic and replaced by one sheep farmer, his shepherds, and 8,000 sheep.

"I do not much like extermination carried out so thoroughly and on system;—it seems bad policy; and I have not succeeded in thinking any the better of it though assured by the economists that there are more than enough people in Scotland still. There are, I believe, more than enough in our workhouses—more than enough on our pauper rolls—more than enough muddled up, disreputable, useless, and unhappy, in their miasmatic valleys and typhoid courts of our large towns; but I have yet to learn how arguments for local depopulation are to be drawn from facts such as these. A brave and hardy people, favourably placed for the development of all that is excellent in human nature, form the glory and strength of a country;—a people sunk into an abyss of degradation and misery, and in which it is the whole tendency of external circumstances to sink them yet deeper, constitute its weakness and its shame; and I cannot quite see on what principle the ominous increase which is taking place among us in the worse class, is to form our solace or apology for the wholesale expatriation of the better.

"It did not seem as if the depopulation of Rhum had tended much to anyone's advantage. The single sheep farmer who had occupied the holdings of so many had been unfortunate in his speculations, and had left the island; the proprietor, his landlord, seemed to have been as little fortunate as the tenant, for the island itself was in the market, and a report went current at the time that it was on the eve of being purchased by some wealthy Englishman, who purposed converting it into a deer forest."

There had always been deer in Rhum, although they had declined and were reckoned to number only some four score at the peak period of the island's cultivation. Thereafter they had the island virtually to themselves for a long time up till the war of 1939. Rhum was for awhile the property of a number of landlords, each with his shooting lodge, until the whole estate was united again under the present owners. During the late war they were compelled to let some of the grazing; and since then it has carried sheep and also a few cattle, besides the deer. The Rhum breed of Highland ponies, small neat nags, has always been maintained. *Mirabile dictu* there are no rabbits on either Rhum or Muck.

Rhum rears itself out of the sea with an imposing array of

mountains, rising to over 2,500 feet, their names echoing Viking
days: Askival, Hallival, Barkeval, Ministral. From the mainland and from Eigg, the mountains are serrated, individual
peaks: from the seaward side and Canna they appear rather
as a vast brooding massif. The coastline is varied, although with
few safe landing places: sometimes a fine greensward down to a
rocky shore, other places are wild and boulder-strewn, and in one
a great cliff of bloodstone plunges into the sea. There is an attractive lodge standing by a loch just above sea level. The geological
formations are of great interest and variety. Almost always along
most of the coast there is a sinister, uneasy swell disturbing
the waters. Only at Kinloch on the east side is there a really sheltered bay and good harbourage provided by Loch Scresort. On
occasion quite large steamers lie in here for shelter from the storm.
There is a wood beside the modern mansion at Kinloch, and
occasional trees in sheltered inlets along the north coast. I remember once sailing along this coast in the company of two farmers
going to the spring sales in long island, one Lowland and one Highland. Rhum has a pretty fearsome appearance and the Lowlander
said with emphasis that it would be a lonely place to live. The
Highlander gazed at a shepherd's house above a little inlet of an
incredible bright green against the tawny moorland, a small but
emphatic oasis of fertility, and said, "No man could be lonely with
such fertile land beside him."

For long visitors have been discouraged from landing on Rhum.
I am in agreement with a neighbouring laird that, in fact, visitors
are what Rhum chiefly needs, and that it would make the ideal
National Park. It has the interest and seclusion of being an island.
It has its ample shooting boxes, which could readily be made
into hostels. The mansion-house itself, lacking in beauty, is well
suited for a large Highland hotel. There is mountaineering, good
walking, stalking, shooting, and fishing in lochs and some fine
little rivers, to say nothing of the sea. The scenery is impressive
and spectacular. It could still carry sheep and cattle, and no dis-
turbance would be caused to its present population—which,
indeed, would have the stimulus of some increase.

35 Stac Skudiburgh, Skye

Canna is an enchanting island, most satisfactorily designed, split in two by a narrow channel, much of it bare at low tide, and so narrow as at one point to be crossed by a long footbridge. The lopped-off part of Canna is called Sanday, a low fertile isle dotted with pleasant croft houses. The main island rises fairly abruptly from the carse opposite Sanday, hills replaced by moorland rising to nearly 700 feet before ending suddenly in cliffs falling sheer to the north. This channel provides good harbourage; on stormy days it sometimes fills with little fishing boats scudding into it for safety, and lying siccar there. Being deep to the east, it has made the construction of a useful pier a comparatively simple job. Men from the drifters decorate the pier and the rock-face behind with the names of their boats and home parts in white and yellow paint. The long stretch of muddy sand and seaweed, uncovered twice every twenty-four hours, makes the strait a good place for birds, duck and waders, and great grey heron. Last, there is something about this schism whereby Sanday is factually but not actually cut off from the rest of the island that makes Canna quite singularly islandlike. Looking from one to the other across the narrow inlet makes one feel pleasantly perched over the sea, sufficiently supported by land, but not earthbound at all, but jaunty with the waves' movement.

The laird's house is handsome and stands over the channel, facing south, sheltered by the bluff to the north, looking at the water between boles of well-grown trees. It has a good walled garden and in spring the wooded policies are lit with daffodils. There is a second, smaller, unhandsome mansion, perched above, more exposed but with fine views to Rhum and back to the long outline of Skye. An agreeable steading stands on the road that runs along the carse towards the bridge. Beyond this the scene changes. Sanday comes to an end. The higher part of the main island transfers itself to the south, with a bay of white shell sand replacing the cliffs to the north. There is good arable land about the mansion-house, and Canna has a famous sheepstock.

Both Daniell and Pennant's engraver depict Canna with the prison prominent. It is a picturesque feature, this little gaol on the top of a round tower of rock that abuts into the sea at the eastern end of the island: it was built by one of the Clanranald chiefs for his wife to prevent her from eloping with the Macleod—unsuccessfully. It is a fair scramble to get up to it, the walls are ruinous, the bright grass on the top ends in space, the last clumps masking a sheer fall into the sea: it is lovely and frightening up there on a still day, with the sea broken with high rocks and reefs and bounded by the curve of a sandy bay. The cliff scenery to the north is splendid, and when there is no swell can be visited in a small boat, passing between pillars of rock, amongst protesting shags and screaming terns and gulls, with a herd of goats feeding on grassy patches far above.

Sanday itself (36) is dominated by an unexpectedly large stone church, not at all in the native style and dedicated to St. Edward the Confessor, although of old the Canna dedication was to St. Columba, who came to Canna in person. Like other of the lesser islands Canna belonged to the Abbacy of Iona until the Reformation. There is an old burial ground and what is reputed to be the ruins of a convent. In penal times the great Father Duggan, sent to the Hebrides by St. Vincent de Paul, included Canna in his mission, which extended from Moidart to Uist. The native population is today entirely Catholic, although there is a small Presbyterian church with a quaint little round tower in the Irish style. The total population is about forty: in Pennant's time it was 220.

Of Eigg, the last of the Small Isles, it is for me at once easy and difficult to write. It has been my home for the last five years. I have known it in winter, spring, summer, and autumn, in all moods, not only its moods of sun and storm, gale and mist, but all my own moods too, which are as variable; and when one lives in a place moods can be contrapuntal—one can be inappropriately sour on fine days and serene in gargantuan rains. I have been involved in Eigg and I have been detached from Eigg: I have doted on Eigg and been bored on Eigg (but "bored" is hardly the word, "disjaskit" is better: one does not get bored on islands—exacerbated, scared, or desperate, perhaps, but not bored; time goes too quickly for boredom, preternaturally quickly). I have ceased to be conscious of Eigg about me. I have been surprised, sometimes, to hear people who have visited many of the islands saying that they thought that Eigg was the most beautiful of them all. It is not, of course, that one becomes indifferent to the beauty of the place in which one lives, only less commonly conscious of it: it has ceased to be primarily a beguilement of the eyes and has become a part of one's daily being. One compares not this place with another, but this place with itself on another day. One is far less conscious of it, but far more immersed in it. The different tempo is less remarkable because one has set one's own pace by it.

Of the people of Eigg I had heard it said before I went there, "they are very kind people", and this by Highland standards. It has been proved for me and my family.

Eigg draws attention to itself from afar. From the mainland it is kenspeckle, the abrupt Sgurr to the south and the long flat slope to the north: I have heard it compared to an aircraft carrier seen forenenst the vast battleship of Rhum. From the south, from Mull and Coll, the slope of the Sgurr is like huge primæval vertebræ. But from close in, by the little inadequate harbourage formed by Castle Island (which never had a castle but is misnamed after a giant who lived there long ago), the Sgurr is breathtaking: a huge perpendicular cone of polished basalt on top of a green hill. It is one of the most weird and arresting and curiously lovely of Nature's freaks. Not like any hill or mountain—too abrupt, and too isolated for a cliff, too massive for a rock: it is simply the Sgurr of Eigg and hardly otherwise to be described at all. But it is only from this frontal aspect that it is spectacular: it is almost disappointing to find later that there is a quite ordinary slope giving access behind.

Eigg has made few impacts upon any history other than its own private history and when it has done so it always seems to be tragically, which is surprising in the case of an island of an exceptionally happy disposition.

Its known history starts with martyrdom. St. Donnan, a contemporary of St. Columba but of the Pictish community, and his Companions were put to death by Vikings presumably, but legend has it that a woman was involved, some Amazonian island queen. So Eigg has its own patron in the Calendar of the Universal Church. Nearly a thousand years later the island makes claim on history with a massacre. There are confusing elements in this story, so much that there is some conjecture that there may have been two massacres taking place within a hundred years or so of one another. However, the story of that massacre of 1577 seems to be as follows. A boat's crew of Macleods from Skye committed rape on some girls of Eigg. They were caught, and mutilated, and sent back in their boat. A vengeful fleet of boats came out from Skye. The people of Eigg, knowing they were outnumbered hid themselves in a cave in the cliffs at Galmisdale. The Macleods searched for them in vain, and at last put to sea again. A spy was sent from the cave to see what was happening but was spotted from the boats, which put back to shore. The man fled to the cave. But a light covering of snow having fallen he was traced by his footsteps. It was impossible for any man to come out of the small entry to the cave in the face of armed resistance. The Macleods piled brushwood against the cave mouth, fired it, and suffocated 395 people, men, women, and children. It is said that one Eigg family, being Macleods themselves, took shelter in another cave, at the north end of the island, and survived; some of their descendants still live in Eigg.

The massacre cave is at the foot of a low cliff by the sea, facing Muck and Ardnamurchan Point. One has to double up to enter it, but after two or three yards it opens out into a capacious rock chamber. Without a good torch, or, better, a flaring brand, one sees nothing except utter darkness. However brightly the sun shines on the water outside, no light penetrates into the massacre cave: it is like darkness softly materialised, as though the whole cave were stuffed with black wool. The bones of the MacDonalds were gathered together and buried during the last century, although even now some fragments have been picked up. It is not, curiously, a gloomy or sinister place, leaving chiefly that impression of profound, almost tangible darkness. A little along the shore from the massacre cave there is a very beautiful cave

36 Canna: crofts on Sanday, looking to the Isle of Rhum

78

with a huge, high vaulted entry, called the Cathedral cave, an obvious name from its noble appearance, but perhaps associated also with its use by the Catholics during persecution days. The high entry continues for some distance; looking back one has a beautiful view of the Hebridean land and sea framed in rock. A steep slope leads up to the inner low-roofed chamber, terminating in a natural apse where Mass was said by the priests who came to the Isles under threat of death. The floor of this natural chapel is now covered with fragments of broken rock, but beneath it is quite even.

The next historical appearance of Eigg is in 1746, when on a June day the relentless Hanoverian net closed upon twenty-five, or according to one report thirty-eight, men of Eigg. Captain Robert Duff of the *Terror* and the notorious Captain John Ferguson of the *Furnace*, sloops, came to Eigg to apprehend Dr. John MacDonald, Kinlochmoidart's brother, who was in hiding there and who had been out in both '15 and '45. The minister of Rhum was on the island at the time and, acting in good faith, persuaded Dr. MacDonald to give himself up in order to prevent action being taken against the Eigg people on his account. Captain Ferguson then asked Dr. MacDonald to tell the men of the island to come to the shore to surrender all their arms, under his guarantee that if they did so their persons and property would be safe. But as soon as Dr. MacDonald had complied he was put under hatches, and when the unsuspecting islanders arrived and gave up their arms all those suspected of having been in the Prince's service were made prisoners. Eigg was ravaged, the women raped, and even the shellfish beds of Laig, an important item of the island's subsistence, were ploughed up so that to this day there are hardly any shellfish to be found in the bay. The young men were transported like beasts to the plantations of Jamaica.

Compared with the massacre, deed of bloody brigandage, this officially sanctioned act is the more vicious. When the forces of law and order become lawless and disorderly the effect is more destructive and socially disruptive than mere feuds, just as the American bandit is a social ill, but not, like Hitler or the Russian

6*

Government, a human disaster. English people are inclined to smile at the freshness of the memory in which Scots often hold the Rising of the '45. It is easier for them to forget the terrible scourge of treacherous hatred with which their troops savaged a great part of the Highlands in 1746. To this day stories, and songs also, which have never been written down, have been passed on from father to son, telling poignantly and immediately of those days. The tendentious verdict of the great Whig historians of the last century who, with stodgy naïvete, recorded the '45 as the last struggle of barbarism against irresistible civilisation, was too easily accepted by an age that complacently closed its eyes to the stews of industrial slumdom. In fact the Hanoverian forces represented amongst other things the *avant-garde* of that same neo-barbarism that threatens the whole world today. I think that taking everything into consideration, and remembering the great sweep on Industrial Progress that it portended, it was in fact a less-civilisation destroying something more nearly related to the primal Christian civilisation. It is impossible to compare the extraordinarily orderly and generous conduct of the Jacobite forces with the deliberately instigated savagery of the Hanoverians without feeling that the conclusions of the Whig historians are inapplicable. Dr. Johnson, for all his lack of predilection for the Scots, would have agreed. Time has marched on; abandonment to material progress has been seen, too late, to lead to nemesis; the victors of the '45 cannot now be represented as the forces of light.

The next phase was, of course, the outcome of the last: that to which Dr. Johnson applied in deep disgust and indignation as he saw island acres already being emptied, "they make a wilderness and call it peace". Most of the people of Eigg were cleared from the land. In 1853 the MacDonalds had to sell. The new proprietor, in order to stock the island with sheep, cleared all the families from the main centre of population, the village of Gruline lying in the shelter of the Sgurr, facing the southern sea. It is a lovely site, occupied today only by one empty shepherd's cottage, the green land eaten up by a monstrous growth of bracken—out of which I once started an eagle, close by me, huge and brown, momentarily like a calf with wings before it took shape and soared up by the gleaming Sgurr. The remaining people were given holdings in Cleadale on flat land (that must then have been very wet and is now going back with drains broken and choked), beneath an astonishing inland cliff. This cliff, rising up to a thousand feet, is of a soft conglomerate rock. Hazel bushes grow up it and innumerable starlike primroses that flower for most of the year—even in winter one finds a plant in bloom here or there in a sheltered spot.

Cleadale stretches between two bays. Laig Bay is a splendid stretch of sand that can look quite white, but is actually a dull grey only enhanced by a thin covering of shell-sand, except when gales blow the lighter shell-sand right away. Cliffs intervene between Laig and the singing sand bay, in Gaelic *Camus Sgiotag*, which is more accurate, for they squeak rather than sing, uttering when they are dry and one walks along them. There are very pleasing rock-divided coves here, with some rock pools that get kindly warm in the sunshine. The sand is a cream colour, rather coarse and crystalline, and the noise, I suppose, is caused by the abrasion of the crystals upon one another. It is something like the noise made when one takes a walk in new corduroy trousers. A second curious characteristic of this sand is that it is seasonal. In winter the seas commonly suck it away, leaving a denuded bed of rock; but, as though mindful of those few persons who visit the bay in the summer, in the spring they bring the sand back again.

North of the singing sands there is a desolate rocky coast, but quite beautiful in sunshine or in tremendous storm with breakers and white-showing reefs, and always the ornament of Rhum beyond.

There is an attractive modest church in Cleadale; rather surprisingly it has a fine mediæval German crucifix and a large sorrowful *Pieta* by Zurbaran. It stands very close to the shore at Laig Bay and its peace is always gently broken by the sough of the waves, most restless of the manifestations of divinity. In Dr. Johnson's day all the people were Catholic, but later Protestant families were introduced and the population is now about half-and-half, living together on the best of terms, it being now nearly half a century since the last tiresome evangelical tub-thumpers from the south came to disrupt the island charity, causing, *inter alia*, a great old fiddler to sell his Cremona violin to a tinker for ten shillings, and eat his heart out for the want of it ever after. The Presbyterian church is on the east side of the island, beyond the school, store, and post office which stand together halfway along the four miles of waterbound, but largely unbound, road. There is a side road leading off by the school to Kildonan, with the ruins of the old church and a fine Celtic cross: a very pretty place with a burn and trees and a view across the Sound to range upon range of the mountains of Morar and Knoydart.

Wildflowers light the island in summer; primroses and flags, orchises, bluebells, wild hyacinths in dense masses, bedstraw, tormentil, corn marigolds, kingcups, meadowsweet, sweet briars and Burnet roses, honeysuckle, stonecrops, and all the little bright flowers whose names one never knows. Autumn empurples the moorland and the scent of heather hangs across the road on still days. Domesticated flowers flourish if they are given shelter from the winds. Hydrangeas do extremely well, and clematis and other flowering shrubs; roses and chrysanthemums and daffodils flourish. On the east side there are plantations and well-grown trees, with dragon's-blood palms in the policies of the mansion. Frost hardly ever gives trouble. If it comes it is in dead of winter, when the shoots are sapless. I little expected it, but I never had such skating as I had in Eigg early in 1947. For seven weeks the lochs were bearing, wonderful marled, glass-like ice. I skated up the length of Loch Beinn Tighe towards the west, where a narrow rim of land holds the waters back from falling into the sea hundreds of feet below, and across the sea Rhum rides at perpetual anchor. I skated on the little loch on top of the cliffs when a crimson sunset made the ice like frozen blood and the sea at my feet below flowed in blood around the Cuillins of Skye. Then there is a lovely deep black loch where the ice was most beautiful and the whipping cracks it gave echoed from enfolding hills. I do not suppose I shall ever again have such skating. Other occasions I remember. A night of full-moonlight, summer-lightning and merry dancers all scintillating together. An eighty-mile-an-hour gale keeping all the island confined uproariously in the school celebrating a wedding with song and dancing. Hot August days surf-riding on the beach at Laig. A desperate rash climb with two small boys after gulls' eggs we never found: rather a gruelling experience that. Bringing a sailing dinghy round by Gruline on a day of November sunshine, the sheet lightly tugging one's hand until, round cliffs, sudden squalls swung the boom across. Fishing for mackerel and saithe in the bay, with all the varying lights on the water, and ugly dogfish snapping at one's line and scarifying the other fish.

The bird-life is not, on the whole, so interesting as that of Canna. But on the inland cliffs the Manx shearwaters breed, as they do on Rhum and, now, on Canna. A remarkable bird the shearwater, only coming inland with its uncanny cries when it is too dark for it to be seen, spending its life far out over the ocean, borne by long wings. Its single young, left to mature and grow hungry by itself in a burrow, used to be a popular article of diet, a rich, oily food: hence probably the error of the Dean of the Isles who credited Eigg and Rhum with solans, whose young likewise were once popular fare. Lately ornithologists have taken shearwaters from Eigg to investigate the peculiar nature of their crepuscular eyes.

Although Eigg figures little in the wider history of Scotland, every part of it has it stories, still remembered by a few people, stories whose treasuring gives a stability and a culture to a society, the strength of tradition and the honour of responsibility. But space presses and I must leave Eigg astern and go over the narrow strip of sea to Skye.

V

Skye has been as much written-up as Iona: Flora MacDonald, Dunvegan, the MacCrimmons, the Cuillins, all are richly docu-mented and need no reintroducing. For myself, although I have seen the familiar outlines of the Cuillins and Talisker and Dunvegan Head recurrently in that time, I have not set foot on Skye for the better part of twenty years. Yet it was the first of the Hebrides that I visited, and I once lived in a crofter's house in Bracadale for a year.

. I went first to Skye because one of my ancestral homes was there, Coirechatachan, where my MacKinnon forebears entertained first Pennant and then Johnson and Boswell. The original Coirechatachan where "we were treated with very liberal hospitality, among a more numerous and elegant company than it could have been supposed easy to collect", is a ruin now, and the male line of the family long resident in Melbourne, Australia; the present Coirechatachan by the shore at Broadford being a later building. There is a story, not recorded by Boswell or Johnson but handed down in the family, that when Corrie's wife asked the Doctor what he thought of the *Scotch Broth* he replied, "Good feeding for swine", to which she responded with alacrity: "Then you will take some more, Mr. Johnson." The entertainment at Coirechatachan seems to have been excellent, with Dr. Johnson in amiable mood, and Boswell joining in the singing with what Gaelic he had, drinking too much punch, and awaking "at noon, with a severe head-ach . . . . About one he came into my room and acosted me, 'What, drunk yet?'"

Skye is a great tattered island stretching for some fifty miles, bitten into by long sea lochs so that no point is five miles inland. It has, in the Cuillins, the most spectacular of all the island scenery (37): the great slagheaps of the Red Hills, monumental, rainwashed into smooth piles of utterly ancient time-crushed rock, and the fine hard, jagged outlines of the Blue Hills, 3,000 feet of the roughest climbing in Britain. Imposing outlines of the Cuillin decorate the view from all airts, relieving desolate stretches of wet moorland or giving a background to fine things on a smaller scale. These are many enough: bays of sand or smooth pebbles, reef-varied seascapes, cliffs of all kinds, shores strewn with vast boulders and slabs of rock, even with small fragments of ancient crumbling coral from long-dead coral reefs, croft houses in little quilted squares of oats and root crops, varying greens and yellows.

I think what I enjoyed best in Skye when I was young was the bathing we had and that, with the sensuous stimulus of water cooling the skin, sharpened one's awareness of the surroundings. It was of all kinds: little peat-moted gold-watered lochans in the hills, remote places rarely seen by men even in the days when Skye was far more thickly populated; water-courses flowing down steep, narrow glens of great greenness, primrose-flecked, with waterfalls and potholes. Then there was the sea bathing. Of this I remember best Oronsay in Bracadale, a tidal peninsula linked to the land by a strand of smooth pebbles like large eggs. Here there are caves and arches of rock, rock shelves with pools of water that grow warm in the sun, some ground out in deep bowls by pebbles swirling inside them, some shallow pans, coloured pink or white, some filled with sinister jungles of weeds. It was a wonderful place to sport, down below the low cliffs of Oronsay on a brilliant summer day, with the warm water of pools and the hot sunbaked rocks, ice-cold water flowing in the deep gullies one had to cross to reach further sunlit ledges or the chill dark of archways and caves. On those days the water beyond, forenenst the high cliffs of Talisker, would be a dancing blue with white terns dip-diving and white gannets plunging. On a November day I rowed with the crofters to the neighbouring small island of Wiay to bring back sheep pastured there for the summer. One sheep had fallen over the cliffs but had made land and was living on the patch of herbage along a precipitous ledge. We chevied it until it fell into the sea, and, a deadweight of water-logged wool, was hauled aboard. Then we gathered the remainder of the flock, wild, mountainy brutes that gave us many spills as we coralled them amongst the rocks by the one landing-place before they were embarked and taken back, a heavy pull for the men on the long sweeps. In the spring I went with a friendly Seceder missionary down to Sligachan, then through the pass, up the fine glen, making a detour to visit Loch Coruisk in its sombre mountain-happed remoteness, until we reached Elgol.

Here my friend bought a score or so of stirks during a long day on which the little beasts were brought, with much excitement and noise, from outlying crofts. In the evening he gave us a sermon in the local Secession church. Next day we started off early, herding the beasts through the Cuillins, having our photos taken by tourists, and spending the night hospitably entertained by a crofter friend. It was the evening of the following day before we and our beasts straggled wearily down the lochside and the people of Struan came out to inspect and pass judgment. And I remember warm hospitality generously given by a household at Collore when, on my first visit, walking all day through drenching rain, I arrived there and was taken in, warmed, partially dried, and magnificently fed, all from kindness. Yet the day before, over in Broadford, I had been miserably fed and overcharged at a house with a board over the door: "Teas". It seemed to me that when people here gave you anything, they gave everything, there was no stint to their generosity: but if they sold you something, they had very little idea of its commercial value and might overcharge grossly. Hence the confused reputation frequently gained by the Highlander. It is not difficult to see how this has come about. A community that has never had much money has little scale of values to go by, and one or two opulent and spendthrift visitors can set a standard that comes hard upon others of us. Also, of course, the gombeen man, the rather rapacious fellow on the make, is a natural enough phenomenon, with his shop or his lorry or his boat for hire, and today he finds any additional inspiration he may need in the hectic extravagance of State Departments.

Dunvegan Castle is the showplace of Skye, with its Fairy Flag, it legends and trophies. As a building it has been much, and inappropriately, altered from Dean Monro's "stark strength biggit on a craig", architecturally is neither interesting nor beautiful, but it has a fine site and the craig has been the Macleod home since the mid-thirteenth century. Armadale, the Castle of the MacDonalds at the other end of Skye, is entirely of the nineteenth century. Their old stronghold, Duntulm, is a toothless ruin, as is the MacKinnon Castle Maoil, guardian of the straits at Kyleakin.

38 The view from Sgurr nan Gillean, Skye

39 Loch Coruisk and the Cuchullins

From the painting by G. F. Robson

40 A sandy bay looking across from South Harris to the
hills of North Harris

More imposing than any of these is the amazing natural ruin of the Quirang. Here in ancient days a volcano squeezed black basalt through the earth's surface, which now, the softer stone washed away, stands a weathered cluster of great pinnacles and needles, hard basaltic rock projecting from a high greensward sloping steeply to the sea at the far tip of Trotternish, the northmost "wing" of Skye. It stands really at the end of a ridge running like vertebræ along Trotternish, incorporating the Storr and the Old Man of Storr, a sixty-foot high basalt pinnacle—part of the same fantastic formation as the Quirang, the Sgurr of Eigg, and the caves of Staffa; with a break above Portree, the town of Skye.

Opposite Portree (30), the Royal Port of James V, a very modest township standing above a fine natural harbour, a sheltered place with trees, lies the long island of Raasay. Here Johnson and Boswell were admirably well received in the new mansion of Macleod of Raasay, which stands yet and is a hotel. It was a very different reception from the dismal one, so delightfully described in the full text of the Tour, given them by Sir Alexander MacDonald and his lady. ("The difference between that woman when alive, and when she shall be dead, is only this. When alive she calls for beer, when dead she'll call for beer no longer.") Sir Alexander had been educated and married in England and had lost the fine patriarchal courtesy, the generosity and good manners so well exemplified in the chief of Raasay. The Raasay Macleods once disputed the chiefship with Dunvegan. The old woman with whom I lived in Bracadale was a Raasay Macleod and, a Seceder, proud as she was of her line, still shook her head over the dances that were held in the mansion when Dr. Johnson stayed there 150 years before. Boswell has a fine portrait of Mr. Malcolm Macleod of the Raasay family who had helped the Prince to escape and gone to prison for it:

"He was now sixty-two years of age, quite the Highland gentleman; of a stout well-made person, well-proportioned; a manly countenance browned with the weather, but a ruddiness in his cheeks, a good way up which his rough beard extended; a quick lively eye, not fierce in his look, but firm and good-humoured. He had a pair of brogues, tartan hose which came up only near to his knees and left them bare, a purple kilt, a black waistcoat, a short cloth green coat with gold cord, a large blue bonnet with a gold-thread button. I never saw a figure that was more perfectly a representative of a Highland gentleman. I wished much to have a picture of him just as he was. I found him frank and *polite* in the true sense of the word."

Raasay is flanked by two islands—Rona to the north and Scalpay to the south, "a rugged island about four miles in length. Dr. Johnson proposed that he and I should buy it, and found a good school and an episcopal church (Malcolm said he would come to it) and have a printing-press, where we would print all the Erse that could be found."

As usual, Boswell brings an agreeable touch even to such a difficult literary motif as island daydreams. Few of the many writers on Skye have been so happy. *The Winged Isle*, the *Isle of Mist*, has suffered often from saccharinic interpreters. It has suffered too, on occasion, from an even more offensive school, those under-bred travellers who return hospitality with a lofty contempt, rebuking their hosts for lacking the enlightenment of Chelsea or Surbiton. Their books read unpleasantly when new, and if read at all when old, but quaintly, for the latest ideas of literary suburbia date quicker than do those of the Isles. Dr. MacCulloch the geologist was something of a pioneer in this vein. MacKinnon of Corrie responded with a gesture of simple contempt by taking an engraving of MacCulloch to Glasgow and having it reproduced on the bottom of appropriate domestic utensils, which he distributed throughout the island.

Although in many ways fascinating, Skye is a somewhat sad place. The population has declined steadily and continues to do so. Bracken is ubiquitous. Seventy years ago, after some grim Clearances, Skye was the stronghold of the Land League, fighting for crofters' rights. An absurdly apprehensive Westminster Government actually sent warships up to intimidate the "rebels": perhaps a last echo of '45 neurosis. But the movement was followed by two fiercesome religious secessions, the coming-out in turn of the Wee Frees and the Free Presbyterians, the ultimate Seceders.

This was like a long-delayed remote version of the Cameronians and the grimmer sects of the Covenanters, except that it was not so political in its genesis. It is responsible for giving the Skyeman, like the Lewisman, a reputation in other parts for "wildness". These irresilient cramping puritanical persuasions, born of and begetting despair, while tenable even, on occasion, without harm amongst a society leading an extremely simple life, become a menace to the young and active beneath the impact of the conflicting ramifications of modern life. There is no flexibility and little forgiveness amongst the extreme Seceders, so that revolt itself is a desolate business, and he who makes it is sometimes driven into a wilderness of recklessness.

II

THE OUTER HEBRIDES

I

THE main island of Barra is in almost every way different from the island of Skye. Yet there is one sense in which Barra is, inconsequentially, akin to Skye. This lies in its variety. It has nothing of the magnitude of the Cuillins, nothing of the vastness or tremendous drama, of the bleakness of desolation. But within its own scale—and it is little more than a twentieth of the size of Skye—it has extraordinary variety, a cinematic change of scene. It is all highly condensed, and can be seen in the best possible way, namely by walking, in a very short time. Whereas Skye demands a hard week of walking at least, often monotonous, it is an easy-going day's walk to traverse the twelve miles of the ring road that circles almost the whole of the Barra mainland. Yet every few hundred yards the scene changes. There is no other island with such variety in so small a compass.

Generally speaking along the east, south of Northbay, the coast is rocky, but varied by many deep inlets bearing in upon the land at all angles, bright with high tide or all brown-gold slithery seaweed with the water away: little boats afloat or stranded at their moorings. All the way there are houses, not in a solid chain but dotted in groups, or singly, spaced out with occasional wide gaps. Every kind of house. Still, in 1950, there remained one true blackhouse, thatched and chimneyless, lived in and well kept, the old lady's cow tethered outside it, finding grass between the broad-bladed flag leaves. Every kind of transition from the blackhouse is to be seen: houses still thatched but with chimneys; houses still with the batter to the walls and the rounded gables, but now roofed with the less-pleasing tarred felt. There are good earlier

41 Ploughing on the flat, sandy Machair of South Uist: in the background the range of hills to the east

19. Kishmul Castle, the ancient home of the MacNeils, Castlebay, Barra

cottage-type houses, and a new house built for himself by a crofter mainly from driftwood since 1945 in the teeth of opposition from an officialdom more concerned with maintaining regulations than with rehousing, and many new houses built to the æsthetically more unfortunate designs of officialdom. These are often roofed with un- attractive asbestos slats. It is curious that one of these plain buildings should boast a ghost, and usually no other inhabitant, since no one stays there long despite the great demand for houses in Barra.

Most of the variety, going south along this road, lies to seaward, although one is always coming upon the sea at fresh angles, but, passing Ersary and Skallary, Heaval heaves into sight inland, almost the only substantial hill of Barra, 1,260 feet high. It is a shapely, tapering hill, that looks a hill, and also displays itself variously, rising at one point high above trees, and later a raw bluff where the road climbs over its shoulder to afford a sudden exultant view of Kishmull Castle on its island in Castlebay. Then the road descends on to the township of Castlebay, pleasantly set around its sheltered harbour. Kishmull, the ancient home of the MacNeill chieftains, rises sheer from the sea at high tide, with just a frill of seaweed round its base when the tide is out (42). The walls look as though they were harled with sea-salt. On the rising ground above the pier a large Catholic church tower domin- ates over the huddle of houses below, beyond it a short distance a good hotel. Then the road inclines north again, cutting off the high promontory of Doirlinn and coming to the bays of white shell-sand sometimes wind-spilt over the turf and the road itself, so breathtaking to those who visit Barra for the first time, or, in- deed, for the hundredth time. The shell-sand has the slightest hint of gold to it, and the Iona green is liberally splashed in all kinds of patterns in the different bays, emphasised by the white surf of the western waves. Here in a little solitary house with a tremendous view lived that great personality and Gaelic scholar, Father John MacMillan. Now the road turns inland, short-cir- cuiting the top of the main bulk of Barra. Here by Greian is the most fertile part of the island, where during the last century the proprietors planted Protestant crofters in an unsuccessful effort to displace the Catholics, who remain the vast majority of the population. The road passes the little kirk, now with a very small congregation, and almost paddling along a loch, gives a fine view across the indented, complicated coast of Northbay, then descends by a wind-cropped wood to Barra's second township. Another of Barra's notable personalities is the postmaster of Northbay, Coddie MacPherson.

Barra may be approached in various ways, each with its own introduction. The mail steamer comes from Oban to Castlebay. That was how I first came to Barra, on a day of winter sunshine, with the dead herbage making the isles an ethereal gold, with long, soft shadows cast by the low sun. I have come also from the north, by small boat from Eriskay, past Fuday, its green as though sprinkled with sulphur with the clusters of primroses that flower in the spring, coming in at the old stone harbour of Eoligarry, the long northern promontory that breaks the compactness of Barra and is joined to the main part by a strip of vegetation between the two stretches of shell-sand, the Traigh Vais and the Traigh Mhor. And this is the middle way of coming to Barra, to land on the Traigh Mhor at low tide by aeroplane. This way, on a day of low cloud, you see least of all. On a day when the pilot reports "visibility unlimited" the eye is filled with the glory of the Hebrides mapped below one on a boundless carpet of blue. Rising from Tiree, Tiree and Coll fall below one, very flat in the water. Rhum, Canna, Muck, Eigg hoist themselves into view against the long backcloth of Skye. A blue world, above, below, to either side: one notices with surprise how far Skye encroaches across the Little Minch. Then the blue land beyond becomes darker, turns green, with vivid gold splashes of sands. Barra, unutterably neat and toylike, bursts into being beneath, familiar landmarks jump out and drop away, the plane comes low over the Northbay school and the Northbay church, then losing height in a couple of turns, comes down across the stretching flat expanse of sand. A sophisticated-looking young lady, with American airline labels plastered over her suitcase, bursts into a flow of Gaelic to the young man at the airport. A cluster of women, very much croftfolk, with scarfs over their heads, see two of their number on to the plane for Benbecula.

I arrived once like this on Ascension Day and walked along the characteristic variegated Barra road, marvelling at the changing scene, reaching Northbay just as the people came out of church, gay and laughing in the sunlight, greeting me as they passed. As I watched them gathered in knots, from the door of the post office, I felt another world join with the palpable Hebridean world about me, the world of France and Italy. Here in Barra there is appreciable that older European tradition from which we in Britain have been much cut off, first by the Reformation, then increasingly by Industrialism. While in those islands whose spiritual life has been impoverished by the firm closing of church doors except on Sundays, and the prim deliberate refusal to smile within the church precincts, for all their loveliness and the goodness and kindness and character of their people, there is a terrible lack, and a cutting off from the great and glorious tradition of the Christian civilisation of Western Europe. So Barra struck me, as I know it has struck other people, as enshrining something desperately precious to a world living under the Terror of the Human Revolt. I remembered the first time ever I visited the island, coming out of church with the Coddie, and his saying to me that he was going to visit an old man who was dying, asking me to come with him. I demurred, convention-hagged, thinking this an odd time to be visiting someone I had never met. "Why not?" he protested, "We all go the same way." So I went with him, up to the little house at the head of the slope, and was welcomed with smiles and privileged to be present at a very happy deathbed, that of a beautiful old man, his grey beard flowing over the neatly turned sheet, and his wrinkled eyelids, when, for a moment, he raised them, revealing eyes of an intense Hebridean blue, the eyes of a sailor. "He knew this coast better than any man," said the Coddie as we came away, "I would always take his advice."

Barra no doubt owes much of its irresistible vitality to the fact that it, alone of all the isles of Scotland, has not a declining population but an increasing one. Agriculturally the land is poor, and

the local fisheries have suffered from the general despoliation by
privateer trawlers and ring-netters, but the majority of the young
men go to sea as merchant sailors, returning often, helping their
families on the crofts, and generally settling at last at home. There
are over 2,000 people on this small island. A remarkable thing is
that, despite occupation by Forces in the war, an increasing
popularity with tourists, the visit of a unit making the film *Whisky
Galore*, Barra remains extraordinarily unspoilt. No doubt many
things have changed in recent years, by no means all for the better,
but the island life has the vigour to maintain its essential qualities
and its Gaelic tongue. In this, of course, Catholicism has been the
great bulwark, with its universality, its roots in essentials and its
ability to touch life at so many points. Many of the people in
other islands belong to those narrow schismatic Churches for
whom so much is sin, or savours of sin. Their beliefs at their best
are by no means despicable, but they as fatally vulnerable. They
have no terms on which to meet modern values. Now it does
not matter how trashy most of those values are, they are in the
air; remote islands are no longer isolated from them. The life
of the Seceder, which, when not made bitter by some canting
preacher, could be admirable and quite secure in a little world
surrounded by stormy waters, now suffers from challenges to
which he has no answer save to reject uninspected, or, if he is
young and adventurous, to accept all too trustingly. Unbending
Calvinism is always inclined to break: the young, in revolt, to
desert an uncomplying creed and its supporters, and to behold
the Hebrides only sentimentally from the dubious comfort of
Glasgow or beyond. Of course, not all Catholic islands are so
favoured as Barra in being able to retain their populations, but
they share something of her resistance to the more confounding
shocks of current stupidity.

Today only one other of the lesser islands of the Barra group is
inhabited, this is Vatersay, the largest and most accessible, lying
as it does across the Sound from Castlebay. Vatersay was raided
by land-starved crofters in 1906, and, after many difficulties and
the imprisonment of some of the crofters, their determination

gained the day and the island was purchased by a reluctant Government for smallholdings in 1909. Ten years later, after the 1914 war, the Barra crofters raided the land at Eoligarry, and here again the Government was ultimately moved to do justice and to legalise their tenure. It was at Eoligarry that the MacNeill chiefs had their last residence in Barra, a curious mansion with a half-basement, something like a townhouse of the late eighteenth century; today it is rather dilapidated, its walled garden forlorn, but the dining-room is now used as a chapel.

South of Vatersay stretch the islands of Flodday, Sandray, Pabbay, Mingulay, and Berneray with its lighthouse, terminating in the bold cliffs of Barra Head. Mingulay is the largest, a fertile island but suffering from the lack of a good landing (44). Once in old times, no one having come for some time to the Barra mainland from Mingulay, the MacNeill sent a boat to investigate. One man, MacPhee, went ashore, and found that the whole population had died of the plague. When he shouted this information to his companions in the boat they refused to take him aboard for fear of infection, and put off home to report to MacNeill. The unfortunate MacPhee was left for a year and a day, the only living soul amongst the corpses on Mingulay. Hardy fellow he must have been, for he survived this ordeal, escaped the plague, picked a living for himself, probably largely of shellfish and seaweed, and was rewarded with a good grant of land on Mingulay when it was resettled. The hill facing north, where he would sit watching for a boat to come to relieve him, is called after him. Mingulay was eventually evacuated, chiefly because of its difficult access. It is now used for grazing and the descendants of MacPhee have returned to the Barra mainland. Fuday and Fioray lie off to the north of Eoligarry, while at the entrance to Northbay there is a whole cluster of little islands centred on the Sound of Hellisay and what is known as the Bishop's Strand, the place of a hundred havens —very beautiful, I am told, and I hope I may sail to them all some summer's day.

Barra takes its name from St. Barr, who was thought at one time to have been a mythical, or at least uncanonised, saint, but is now generally identified with the Irish St. Finnbar. The final *a* is, of course, the Norse monosyllable denoting island, the *I* in Iona, and *a* or *ay* in so many suffixes. It suffered comparatively late from that process that overtook all the Islands and Highlands, whereby the laird, as Dr. Johnson expressed it, became instead of a chief "a trafficker in land", with great impoverishment of his people. The cosy-thoughted of the nineteenth century saw it as a fruit of sublime ineluctable progress, whereas, in fact, if by force of exterior circumstance the clan system had to go, it was not being superseded by something superior but only destroyed by forces intent upon the assertion of new irresponsible values, those forces of materialism that ever assert themselves against systems based, howsoever incompletely, upon truer values. The last MacNeill proprietor, in financial straits himself, began the abuses before he was dispossessed by his creditors in 1827. Thereafter far into the nineteenth century there was an increasing poverty, emigration, evictions, even enforced transhipment across the Atlantic. The successive Crofters' Acts slowly restored some rights of tenure, and coupled with the initiative and courage of land-raiders, made living conditions possible again and so today Barra stands, a small rock against seas more ferocious than the Atlantic, the breakers of contemporary chaos.

Between the Barra Isles and Uist lies Eriskay of the love lilt, the barest of lands, yet more densely peopled than any other island. There really seems to be hardly any earth on Eriskay at all. Down by the shore potatoes and patches of oats grow in what looks like pure sand, sustained by quantities of seaweed dug into it. The only enclosures are the dykes round the old and the fence round the new cemetery, and the fence that surrounds Ben Scrien, the 609-foot hill of Eriskay, where the ubiquitous rock is in some places topped by the thinnest possible layer of peat, sprouting heather and coarse grasses, the common grazing for the island bull and the many white ponies, with their little black foals, which, with hazel panniers on their backs, serve as the pack-horses for every burden on this wheel-less, roadless island (45). It would be hard to find another island so barren, yet more than 400 people live on this rock, exposed to every winter gale, enwrapping mist, or streaming downpour. The land seems utterly uncomplying: the weather can be all-suppressing. Yet in contrast and divine compensation it would be difficult to see any view in the world so beautiful as that from Eriskay on a fair day of summer. From the slopes of Ben Scrien one looks over a sea of indescribable butterfly-wing blues and Iona greens, islands and the Uist shore rising golden from it beyond a chain of little sandy bays each with its tidemark of pink shells, and, passing along the coast, the shapely red sails of the boats going to set their lines for flatfish.

There are great gaps in the known history of Eriskay, since a forgotten Viking, Eric, gave it his name. Down on its little satellite islands to the south, the Stacks, stand the remains of Weaver's Castle, a corruption of Reiver's Castle from the piratical gentle-man who built it. There seems to have been quite a large popula-tion when the first Vicar Apostolic to Scotland, Bishop Nichol-son, visited it in 1697. But thereafter there must have been a decline or an evacuation, for, in 1745, when Prince Charles Edward made his first landing on Scottish soil in the lovely bay, the southernmost of the little chain of sandy bays, that bears his name and alone grows the pink convolvulus whose seed is supposed to have fallen from his pocket, fresh from France, there were only a few herds living on the island. It only became repopulated about a hundred years later, and populated just because it was so barren a place. Some of the newcomers came, refugees, from Barra. Most of them came from South Uist, people who had already been evicted first from the fertile Machair, being put to live behind Ben Mhor until by their husbandry they had made that fertile, and the tacksmen put them on to the still poorer land of Bagh Hartavagh. When they had made that worth the tacksmen's taking over, they were chased over the Sound to Eriskay, so profitless a place that they were left there in peace. Possessed only of such inadequate holdings they became chiefly dependent upon the fishing. Within living memory they could catch all they needed with sailing boats or even rowboats, close in to the islands. Since then the unchecked spoliation of the waters has driven the fish farther and farther from the shores, and now few Eriskaymen can afford powerful enough boats for the net-fishing, so another vigorous flourishing population has started to decline and only two or three boats lie in the fine landlocked harbour on the east side of the island.

Here, along by the harbour, you will find lazy-beds and tiny outcrops of crops hanging between rock and sea. "Fields" of oats, or potatoes, barely three square yards in extent. Visitors from better favoured parts find these determined efforts to cultivate mere handkerchiefs of ground rather odd. But I think it is not so odd. Man has done this for countless years, and, despite the scientists with their shattered millenium in their hands, will do it (unless, indeed, the scientists destroy worldly existence altogether) for countless more. What is really odd is that people should clock in at factories and offices and conduct themselves as they do in our industrial cities. That is really quite a novelty and one that will more likely seem strange to future generations; quaint, hard to understand.

It was between Eriskay and Barra that the famous merchantman *The Politicia* went on the rocks during the war. She carried 23,000 cases of whisky, of which 5,000 cases were salvaged locally and unofficially. I asked the Coddie how he first heard of the advent of *The Politicia*. "I was speaking to the Eriskay schoolmaster on the phone," he told me, "and I asked him how were they all in Eriskay. 'There's been a lot of cases of sleeping sickness here lately,' he said. 'Oh dear,' said I, 'I hope it will not come to Barra.' 'I hope not,' said he, and rang off. But it did come to Barra." *Whisky Galore* was an amusing film, but it seemed thin to those who had tasted of *The Politicia*.

II

Across the gannet-busy Sound from Eriskay, its waters brilliantly lit by sand below and the bowl of sky above, lies the brief south coast of South Uist, the next component of the "Long Isle". Unlike Barra, South Uist is anything but compact. It is, of course, a far larger island, but it is made particularly difficult

43 The Atlantic coast of Lewis: Ard More Mhangusta

44 The great cliffs of Mingulay in the Barra group

45 Eriskay transport: pony with panniers

46 Black houses in North Uist

to get to know by its great length, stretching north and south, bitten into by sea lochs, baulked by mountains, served by little more than one good road with most of the main communities situated some distance from it. This curious arrangement is due partly to geographical causes, partly to the fact that when the road was first made the lairds and tacksmen would not allow it to run along the machair, but just to the east of it. The machair is the long sandy west coast of the Long Isle, particularly remarkable in South Uist—such a tremendous stretch of sandy shore, slightly separated from dead flat fields by low sandhills. These fields form the bulk of the arable land (41). In winter they are the resort of tens of thousands of wild geese, feeding on grass with comfortable cackling and watchful sentries who raise the whole gaggle in a cloud when one approaches too close. The skeins of geese in flight rise and fall across the machair, like beeves of outsize bees. Some of the geese stay to breed in the numerous lochs during the spring, a tribute they hardly pay elsewhere in Britain. An amazing sight at the meeting of winter and spring is the gathering of the tangle where the waves bring it, in huge quantities, along the shore of the machair. Crofters drive their carts right into plunging waters, men and women hectically filling them with the long banner-like tangle, drive the cart back to a cache behind the sand-dunes, then down into the sea again for another load. All is violent, hectic, watery activity, haste and determination, against the gleam of pale sky and the broken lights on the sea.

Today down by Garynamonie there is a factory for processing seaweed, for making such modern essentials as the stiffening for ice-cream, having the advantage of being if not nutritious not actively poisonous. By all means may it thrive, and may it produce truly useful materials, but, since the islanders have suffered from some ignorant criticism for alleged lack of co-operation in keeping the factory supplied with its raw material, perhaps a word or two of explanation is called for. In the first place considerable quantities of seaweed are essential to the fertility of the fields along the machair whose soil is so largely sand. The seaweed harvest, after the winter storms, coincides with the busiest time on the crofts

So long as the crofters continue to put their agriculture first, they are showing a far greater wisdom than the Central Government of Britain. Furthermore, the commercial exploitation of seaweed is no new thing in the Isles, but one that has already brought disaster on an appalling scale. In 1765 kelp-burning was introduced into the Highlands and Islands. It proved highly remunerative to the landlords, who received from £16 to £22 a ton. The crofters received little over £2 a ton for their labour, and in addition had their rents raised. After about fifty years a series of changes in the market brought a sharp slump to the prices given, and in 1822, with the reduction of the duty on barilla from Spain, the industry was abandoned altogether (although in a few places, more particularly in the Orkneys, kelp was subsequently and until quite recently burnt for iodine). This sudden loss of income was an acute impoverishment to the crofters, the more particularly since the landlords suffered likewise. They not only did not reduce the increased rents, but tried various means to recoup themselves for their loss, evicting crofters in favour of tacksmen or sheepfarmers: generally in vain, even from their own point of view, and many estates went bankrupt. While some of the blame for the terrible distress that overtook the Isles and West Highland coast must remain with the lairds, it is a facile and misleading Socialist type of argument to blame them entirely. They too were victims of an industrialised system that had drawn their interests away from their estates and those for whom they were responsible. Paternalism that, even deliberately after the triumph of incipient industrialism in 1746, had been destroyed was, as Dr. Johnson appreciated, the only justification of chiefship. No entirely satisfactory substitute for a responsible leadership based upon overlordship has yet been evolved. But responsibility, always the weak element, was largely destroyed in the industrialising process. Many lairds were busy cutting a dash in the glitter of London, the very symbol of centralisation: they had come to see their properties as merely a means to this new focus. They had lost touch and sympathy.

Uist suffered badly from its landholders; not so much from

Clanranald but from the tacksmen who succeeded. Rather earlier, in 1770, the laird of Boisdale began a veritable persecution of his people. A Catholic, he apostasised and tried to enforce apostasy upon them on penalty of losing their holdings if they did not comply. The walls of the garden into which he once coralled the people and where they resisted his demands still stand, but the mansion he built himself has been demolished to provide stones for the byres of the descendants of those who managed to remain. A great many, however, were evicted and emigrated across the Atlantic, Bishop Hay being successful in raising funds on their behalf. Boisdale died crying out for a priest, a service which his sons denied him.

Boisdale is the southern promontory, where the long road ends at Polachar, with a short branch east to the Eriskay ferry. At Polachar there is an inn, and a shallow loch said to have been walked into existence by the pipers of Uist—and Uist is the great home of piping. The next branch road turns off at Daliburgh, a fair centre with its large church and school, and the homely hospital run by the Sisters of the Sacred Hearts. This road leads to Lochboisdale, important as the port and post town of Uist, with a hotel of famous hospitality. Thereafter for many miles the road drives north, with only rough tracks leading off it, on one side the machair, on the other moorland rising to sizeable hills, and everywhere lochs and lochans, mostly shallow, some islanded, some scattered with water-lilies, bringing scraps of the sky to earth, blue when the heavens are blue or on the long summer twilights colourless, absent, making the world seem slight. The next substantial inlet on the east coast beyond Loch Boisdale is Loch Eynort, and the biggest of the Uist hills lie to the north of it, Hecla and Beinn Mhor which rises over 2,000 feet. It is only really from the air or from the tops of its hills that any comprehensive impression of South Uist is to be gained at all. From the heights the bewildering wilderness of land and water suddenly takes a tattered shape, stretching away to the south with only rather larger stretches of reflecting water separating Eriskay and Barra. To the west the machair ends in a clean line and far out to sea the cliffs of St. Kilda rise solitary in the Atlantic waste. Below the ridge of Beinn Mhor, eastward, the hillside falls drastically, down gullies and chimnies, to two little lochs far below and a green promontory jutting into the sea, the "back of Beinn Mhor", where once evicted crofters made a home and greenness, now deserted. The view of Loch Eynort, with its isles and curves and bays, is fascinating, and coming down on to it one finds a deep gully, filled surprisingly in this windswept land with small but well-grown trees. There is a lovely freshwater loch nearby, with smooth rocky shores broken by sandy bays, and an island golden with royal fern. Only now, in 1950, is something more than a track being constructed to give access to the houses by Loch Eynort, the work being excellently done by local labour.

Across the machair from Loch Eynort, beyond the church at Bornish, there is almost the only projection along the whole straight line of the west coast, Rudha Ardvule. Small as it is, it contains a loch of its own. A little to the north Ormaclett, the ruined castle of the Clanranald MacDonalds, stands kenspeckle across the flat land; and beyond it the substantial crofting community of Stoneybridge. The lodge of the present proprietor of South Uist stands at Grogary, with walls and a few trees huddling to keep a garden against the gales. Opposite it a rough road runs to the last and least of the three big bites into the eastern seaboard, Loch Skiport, an isolated place, its waters deepset and deep, with a small pier used for cargoes for the north part of the island and for Benbecula, which is harbourless. This road runs along the indented shore of the freshwater Loch Druidibeg, with its many islands and secluded reaches where geese nest. Here rhododendrons and big-flowered gorse make a blaze in the summertime.

The last stretch of the South Uist road crosses Loch Bee, largest of all the freshwater lochs, so shallow it can be waded almost anywhere by the fishermen who come for its many trout: it sometimes ships seawater, and flounders and lithe have settled in with the trout. It has often great concourses of swans upon it, and herds of shapely garrons, Highland ponies, feeding on the banks.

South Uist has a population of five or six thousand, about a thousand of whom are Protestant descendants of those introduced by the tacksmen from North Uist. The crofters raided the remaining big farms during and after the 1914 war and were subsequently given holdings by the Board of Agriculture, despite which there was a good deal of emigration in the 1920's. Almost the only fishing now is for lobsters, although boats from afar put in at Loch Boisdale. The seaweed factory has started to use rockweed in the summer when there is little tangle. It is cut from the rocks with a sickle and floated along the shore tied together in "rafts" of about a ton, a day's gathering. The factory should prove an asset to the island, although, of course, it does not constitute a complete local industry; the weed is only processed there into a form convenient for export to the mainland, where it is manufactured into a marketable product. It is a curious fact that very little is known about seaweed and much research remains to be done. It is not known, for example, whether deep-seaweeds have completed their life cycles by the time they come inshore; whether the same weed comes back again and again; how many of the different kinds of weeds are procreated. But the West Highland coast is one of the richest in seaweed. In old days some of it was quite an important article of diet. Dulse can be eaten raw, and may people still put carrageen to good use, drying it and making it into excellent, wholesome puddings.

Between South and North Uist lies Benbecula (48), an island, not a hill but very much the reverse; a complete pancake of an island pockmarked with water holes, lochs and lochans of every size and design, stravaiging everywhere so that it is hard to tell which are of fresh water and which are complicated inlets of the sea. Some bits are broken off altogether and lie, islands and reefs, dotted about off shore, save to the west, where the Atlantic swell grinds everything to sand. Up to the last war communication between South Uist and Benbecula was tidal, and somewhat hazardous at that, by way of the strand of the South Ford, but now at last the ford has been bridged with a long low concrete viaduct (48). The roadway across the ford has always a scattering of broken cockleshells upon it, for the adaptable gulls have discovered in it a convenient anvil for cracking the cockles they gather from the beds nearby.

Lacking that wonderful greensward, Benbecula has not the same breath-taking quality to its flatness as Tiree; besides it is scarred and scored with its waters. Houses, of which there are many, loom unnaturally large and, to those used to the more common enfolding Scottish scene, deceive with apparent proximity, whereas they may be a long gait away, and a hard one if the wind that pours unchecked over the flats is adverse. Quite a short walk may be entirely exhausting, or it may be accomplished with a kind of hilarious effortlessness and lack of dignity, one's body propelled, one's legs swirling about below it, and, often enough, bullets of rain rattling on one's oilskin. So little of it visible at a time, the scenery depends much upon the sky, and often Benbecula lies below weird and splendid clouds with stabs of sunlight or smears of pink and orange towards evening, great hosts and armies of the salted damp that broods upon this outpost of the European mainland. Benbecula claims one hill in Rueval, but there are only 400 feet of it. The best general view is from the air. Rising from the airport at Balivanich in the north-west corner, Benbecula presents an extraordinary confusion of land and water, often half-concealed by low white cloud, bays and rocks and foreshortened headlands, green and gold and peatbrown.

Most of the Benbecula roads lie to the east, where the land is not so raddled with water. Here stands the old eighteenth-century mansion of Nunton, the home of the Benbecula branch of the Clanranald family, who succeeded to the chiefship after the last of the Ormaclett branch was killed at Sheriffmuir. It has a good deal of dignity left to it, and, amongst the various tenants who now live in its handsome old rooms, one notable personality of an eighteenth-century vintage, dealer and singer and dancer and storyteller, Mac Shunndachain.

Benbecula retains much in the way of those old songs and stories, the Hebridean variant of the common heritage of the peasantry of Western Europe. Since the Brothers Grimm made their famous German collection, much has been done, particularly in Sweden and in Eire, to record the tales of the old storytellers. Yet, for some reason, perhaps the richest source left anywhere today is in the Catholic, or dominantly Catholic, Outer Hebrides. One reason for it may be that amongst the Hebrideans, after the abrupt disappearance of Celtic ornamentation at the Reformation, and with the extreme limitations upon domestic decoration imposed by the blackhouse, piping and the weaving and dying of wool apart, song and story were the only artistic outlet left. So that these acquired and maintained a very considerable import- ance. Unfortunately they were for a long while condemned by the Protestant ministers as worldly foibles and untruth, and later subject to renewed attack from the Secession preachers, so that it is amongst the Catholics that they chiefly survive. Right up until the present the *ceilidh* (which means a *visit* rather than an organised social occasion) was the chief form of entertainment. *Ceilidhs* took place in the different houses throughout the winter, and at them stories were told and songs were sung. Quite often, where the size of the population made it practicable, certain formalities were observed: a young man became a regular visitor at one house and did not go to that of any rivals. I know a Barra- man who went as a boy to the same storyteller every winter night for fifteen years and never heard the old man tell the same story twice. To understand this we have to appreciate that in learning how to read we have sacrificed a faculty almost incomprehensible to us now, the faculty to learn word-for-word almost instantane- ously. Yet it was in this manner that so much of the early lore and poetry of all lands was passed down to us, and in remoter parts there are still a few old people who retain the gift and the stories.

There were two chief kinds of storyteller, the *Seanchaidhe*, the historian who preserved the tales of local history with a remarkable precision, for truth was his concern and pride and he rather despised his counterpart, the *Sgeulaiche*, who retailed romantic tales. These latter are of great variety and varying antiquity. There are the tales of the Fionn cycle—the birth of Fionn, the qualifica- tions of the Heroes, Diarmuid with the fatal love-spot on his forehead drawing Fionn's wife, Grainne, to him. Here, in Benbecula, was found the chant on the death of Diarmuid, more than a thousand years old. Many of these tales have probably been committed to manuscript more than once, then, the MSS. being all destroyed, preserved again as oral tales. A separate cycle of Hero tales concerns the Son of the King of Lochlainn. What are known as international folk tales have themes common to many countries: the Perseus and Andromeda motif is one of the commonest, developed with many variations. Bits of Bible stories culled originally from sermons have been adopted, and legends of the childhood of Jesus from the Apocryphal New Testament— the child being hidden under seed on the flight to Egypt, the hen scratching the seed from him, the duck replacing it, so that the hen is accursed and the duck blessed. Animal fables, jokes and anecdotes embroidered and expanded, fairy stories of all kinds, ghost stories, tales of chiefs, of the second sight, all are grist to the mill. There is a whole range of elaborate stories, rather like romantic novels sauced with sorcery, each taking perhaps as long as ten hours in the telling still related by a great old Benbecula *Sgeulaiche*, Angus MacMillan. These stories are amongst those that have lately been recorded by my good and scholarly friend Calum Maclean, a Raasayman working for the Irish Folklore Commission, who have done us a great service in sending him here. But perhaps most of us are most moved by the Gaelic songs with their strange, lovely airs, sung in the old way, unaccompanied, the settings unaltered. Many of these also have never yet been recorded, although they belong to all periods, and may easily be dated by an expert. There are hymns and prayers of great antiquity, and songs of heroes and of historic battles. There are flytings and scurrilous lampoons, often traditionally sung at the waulking of the cloth, when the tweed was shrunk by the lassies working to a rhythmic chant sung by a leader while all joined in the chorus. There are laments and love songs of heartrending sadness.

Benbecula has about a thousand of a population. After Clanranald had refused to convert his people forcibly, the best land

47 The Standing Stones of Callanish, Lewis

48 The bridge built in 1941 across the South Ford between
Benbecula and South Uist

49 Tarbert, Harris: the principal township situated on its narrow neck of land

was given by the ministers and tacksmen to Protestants from North Uist and also from Skye, but there is no bitterness whatever between their descendants, and the population today is about half and half. North Uist itself is entirely Protestant, but considers itself linked to Uist rather than to the Protestant islands of Harris and Lewis to the north. The link will be very properly strengthened, and communications much improved, when the North Ford is bridged, as the South Ford has been. Of course, the North Ford is a good deal wider, but there are islands that can be linked up and the road taken through the substantial and populous island of Grimsay to the east of the ford. At present the crossing is made at low tide by pony traps, always at some risk, at least of a wetting, as there are treacherous sands which shift their position so that even the most experienced driver may be caught, sometimes with the loss of his pony. There is also now a mail-ferry. An antiquated trap, its paint peeled off by the sea and weather, meets the slick, gleaming Dakota that lands at Balivanich, receives the mails for North Uist, rattles off down a superb £20,000 runway (passing close to a blackhouse incongruously supplied with an air-raid shelter), switches to a track, then across wet sands, and the mails are transferred to a motorboat. This boat takes the mails, and any passengers, through the channels of deeper water, past seals and seabirds, to the pier, or at least the rocks of Carinish. Certainly the traps are the gayer mode of transport, inspiriting to see them birl over the sands at speed, pursued perhaps by a couple of dogs who follow them so far just for the trip and scamper back wet and merry, with flecks of foam flying and perhaps a spittle of rain or a scantling of the sand itself.

North Uist (46) is much of a size with South Uist but more compact and tractable and more easily served by roads: even so, the population is rather smaller. It is low-lying but not flat as Benbecula, although flat enough always to reveal its three hills, Eaval, Marrival, and the Lee which has a north and a south summit. They brood over the island graciously, shapes quickly familiar. The east side of the island is tashed and slashed with lochs and inlets, with a pier in Loch Maddy where the mailboat calls. To the west and north there are tidal islands across wide stretches of sand, also Boreray and Berneray, true islands lying to the north. Berneray has a fair population and is a favoured place, but for some reason it is always accredited to Harris, although much closer to North Uist, probably because it was a home of the Macleods. Pabbay, beyond Berneray, had a population until 1840, when the people were put off, nominally for distilling, but in those days the possession of a particularly fertile island by crofters was a more heinous offence. Just at Carinish stands the remains of the *Teampul na Trionaid*, a church of the Holy Trinity rather larger than most of the numerous early church buildings in the Isles. The ruin is roofless and crumbling, but bright with yellow lichens and rather finely situated, overlooking the sands between the Uist mainland and Baleshare, which are like the adjacent sands of the North Ford, not the dazzling white shell-sand but a more ordinary colour. By Paible, the main community along the west coast, the silver-sands show again, in dunes, and the machair starts, brilliant and sweet with wildflowers in the summer.

Along most of the west coast there are attractive well-kept thatched houses of blackhouse type but with chimneys and greater convenience generally (46). They show, in short, the slight modifications which are almost the only changes wrought upon the Hebridean houses in many hundreds of years. Of course, the traditional blackhouse until well into the last century commonly shared its roof with the byre. It was called "black" not from its external appearance but from the blackening of the interior by peat smoke that had no ready egress. It was said, and probably with some truth, that cold and other germs did not easily survive the peat-reek. Externally the houses have a positive "protective colouring", the thatch and the local stone blending so featly with the surroundings, the rock and coarse grasses and heather, that there is commonly too little definition to obtain a good photograph. The thatch was of straw or of rushes or bents. Heather made the longest-lasting thatch, but was the most diffi-cult to work with. In North Uist you will still see drystone walls, and detect the core of sand between the double thickness. In many places, particularly in the Long Isle, there were practically no houses built between those of blackhouse type and those put up under the Board of Agriculture schemes of grants and loans after 1918. These schemes have been of great help in rehousing the people, but there is one quite damnable feature to them. The stock designs were a true work of bureaucracy. They were evolved in distant offices by those with no knowledge either of the Highlands or of architecture. They bear the horrible stamp of the witless technician. The designs are dictated with an entire, positively candid, contempt for æsthetics: they are inspired not even by comfort or convenience, or by building considerations, but simply for conformity to regulations of cubic capacity and window area and ceiling height evolved for the slums and stews and suburbs of London. It is useless to protest that the same requirements do not apply in the Hebrides, that, indeed, the requirements for comfort are very different. Nor to point out that the same technicians, having resolutely insisted that these completely arbitrary measurements were essential to the public health, scrapped them all at a word from the Great God of Mass Production and sanctioned the pre-fabs. Throughout the islands the ugly boxlike structures have gone up, largely built by the crofters themselves, often of excellent craftsmanship crying out for decent design. Only very rarely have crofters been able to modify the officially imposed ugliness, for officialdom holds the money bags and grants are withheld for departure from grim conformity. The stock double-storey tradesman's box with "storm-windows" sits very ill on any landscape. Be it added that the rooms of the upper storey, provided at considerable extra difficulty, and with less protection against storms, by the "storm window", are extremely awkward and cheerless, the low walls being too low for any practical purpose, for which indeed they are not intended, being designed only to supply regulation cubic capacity.

Today in Uist and Benbecula and elsewhere Swedish timber houses are being erected. Not the single-storey houses designed for such parts, but, because they are cheaper, double-storey houses, abrupt and unconforming to the landscape. They have, of course, proved almost unlivable in during the winter gales. It is all part of the thraldom of belonging to an industrialised society with its constant tendency towards uniformity and totalitarianism. How different from countries where building is still an expression of joy in life. Incidentally, it was Swedish architects who, some years ago, made a study of the blackhouse, and demonstrated that much of what seemed primitive was in fact (as might be expected) extremely practical and suited to the prevailing conditions and climate; they suggested ways in which blackhouse forms could be modernised and a pleasing and highly serviceable house evolved. I believe some years ago the present proprietor of North Uist hoped to build to these specifications; one can imagine the dead horror—and complete obstructiveness—with which officialdom would meet such intentions!

III

Whereas North and South Uist are indeed three separate islands but often thought of as one, Harris and Lewis are really one island yet are always regarded as distinct. In fact the people of Harris and Lewis are insistent upon the distinction, and Harris comes under the county administration of Inverness, while Lewis is considered as part of Ross. Nor does the division come at the extremely narrow neck of land between East and West Loch Tarbert (Tarbert incidentally, a common name on the West Coast, is a Viking word denoting a place where a boat could be drawn across from loch to loch or sea to sea), but less perceptibly between the head of Loch Resort on the west and Loch Seaforth, just opposite its island hill, on the east. Tarbert is simply the meeting place of North and South Harris, which are of about equal area, but the North being chiefly the mountains of a deer forest, most of the people live in the South. Of old, Lewis, or the Lews, was wrested from the Macleods by the Seaforth MacKenzies, whereas Harris remained a Macleod property; that may be the dominant reason for the division, but in fact the two places hardly look alike, and there is a difference in the people themselves.

Harris has the more varied landscape. Even the west and east sides of South Harris are extraordinarily different. It is not merely that one has a sandy and the other a rocky coast, but the east coast is surely one of the rockiest inhabited places under the sun. Everywhere rock faces burst through the thin soil: thousands of boulders jostle one another in beds of heather. Rocks mount the hills and guard the shores. There are lochs in bowls of rock. There are hilltops of solid rock. Houses are like rocks animated by occupation, but often hard to distinguish from the blocks of rock around them. There is a fantastic attraction to it all, charming bits of green secluded one from another by knowes and rocks grotesquely weathered. Cultivation is done in lazy-beds (61). Where the name lazy-bed came from, goodness knows; it is no lazy job to till these scraps of soil between rocks, on the edge of bogs and ditches, overhanging the sea. Shape and size dictated by the exigencies of the terrain, the lazy-beds form low humps, rather like the upswelled grass over a new grave, and often no bigger, comprised of the poor earth enriched with dung and seaweed, growing potatoes or oats, flaunting green amongst the barren stones. It may be imagined that they make only a modest contribution to the livelihood of the people. Weaving, at present undergoing a slump, and lobster-fishing are the main employments. In the small island of Stockinish, a stone's throw from the coast, is a sea-loch, of which the mouth has been partially dammed so that it may be used as a store for lobsters. Unfortunately it is several fathoms deep and it has proved harder than was expected to recapture the lobsters when they are required for the market, and the price has been low—a good deal less than that given by an enterprising London dealer who has been flying lobsters south from Benbecula. During the war felspar was mined where a white gash still shows. The seam runs through the island and there is talk of opening another mine. In this poor land all the people are Seceders.

Besides coming in to the pier at Tarbert, the mail steamer makes less frequent calls at Rodil in the extreme south-east corner, where it is met by a ferry boat. At Rodil the stark scene changes. The

loch is amiable, there is a good hotel, and, passing by the, mercifully somewhat concealed, war relics of black Nissen huts, a
most attractive little green strath running along the base of Harris.
The jewel of this strath is the church of St. Clement (51). A first
view of St. Clement's capped tower seen walking over the hill
from Obbe is strangely thrilling. Here some of the green slopes
have big trees on them, and the road winds, enticing, towards
this last, Iona apart, of all the Gothic churches and chapels that
once graced the Isles left not a ruin. How very fine it is, this civilis-
ing impress upon God's beautiful scene, this fit rendering of
thanks: man gracing not disgracing his gifts. Here is one of the
loveliest, because completest, views in the Isles.

St. Clement's is a lovely church by any standards, with its
long low body and tower erect. It is fascinating in its fusion of
Gothic with Celtic design. Set in the tower are vigorous carvings,
heads of a bull and a horse, a galley, St. Clement himself, and
below him two inclined figures, one kilted (50). There is also a
nude figure of a woman squatting, legs apart, phallic. Inside are
three figured tombs, the best of them the Macleod tomb of 1528,
richly carved, with God the Father uplifting the crucified Son,
the Virgin and Child, the twelve Apostles with their names on
scrolls, a galley, a hunting scene, and other devices, inscribed
with Gothic lettering cut in relief. There are sword tombstones
on the floor, and an eighteenth-century slab, also a crucifix,
Celtic, attenuated, spiritual. The church is not used but was well
restored, first by a Macleod owner, then by the Countess of Dun-
more, a subsequent owner of the island. Part of the tower rests on
the naked rock, cut into by it. In the graveyard lies Mary
Macleod, the great Gaelic poetess. There are some handsome
balustraded burial places of the eighteenth century, now inclined
to topple; one hains the remains of a Macleod of Berneray who,
"past the prime of life", killed a dragoon in single combat at the
Battle of Falkirk. This champion of the Stuart cause married his
third wife in his seventy-third year and had nine children by her.
His tomb also records that his grandfather and a grand-uncle
were knighted on the field of Worcester.

The pleasant road from Rodil leads to Obbe, renamed Lever-
burgh at the time of Lord Leverhulme's quaint, pathetic effort
to bring the "civilisation" of Port Sunlight to the Isles. Its architectural medley is now being completed by the erection of Swedish
houses. The Obbe is a much enclosed sea loch; a partly artificial
semi-sea loch leads into it, and into that a freshwater loch fed by
a burn from the big inland Loch Langavat. Artificial runs between
many sea and freshwater lochs in Harris provide splendid sea-
trout fishing. A few miles beyond Obbe below the village of North-
ton there is a high flat traigh of golden sand, brilliant in sunlight,
sore on the eyes, much of it rarely covered by the sea and in season
flushed with sea pinks. It lies flat and desert-like between the 1,201-
foot hill of the Toe of Harris, and Maodal, rising 820 feet from the
shore. The waves here, straining to reach up the sands, are often
very beautiful, green-running, white-frilled. Now the road runs
up the west coast by sandy shores past the Isle of Taransay, which
not long since had a school but now is the home of only one
farmer, to a second great spread of sand, Traigh Luskentyre,
the estuary of the River Laxdale. Lax is a common Norse prefix
in the Isles and signifies salmon or sea-trout. A by-road runs along
the north side of the bay to a few houses and a school that is chiefly
populated by one large family of handsome children whose home
stands superbly situated above a little bay of white sand, seas
running Iona green, looking across West Loch Tarbert to the
splendid mountains of North Harris.

The road that runs from Tarbert along the north shore of the
West Loch passes the old whaling station at Ardhasig. The
buildings are tumbledown, but after twenty years' disuse, in 1950
operations were started there again by the Norwegians, with a
depot ship moored in the bay. They caught their first whale on
June 16th, to the north-west of St. Kilda. Blue and sperm whales
are the quarry, caught for their oil, but every part can be put
to some use, meat, bone, and all. And when whales have given
themselves indigestion by a rash indulgence in shellfish, ambergris
forms in their stomachs, grey, oozy, mudlike, stinking, and
extravagantly valuable as fixing for the most elegant perfumes.

One dyspeptic whale may contain nearly £10,000 worth of amber-gris. The whales are inflated at sea and towed to the depot ship for their rather unsavoury dismemberment.

The roadway winds along the coast underneath the hills, past inlets and the finely situated North Harris Lodge, with it gardens and parapet and rhododendrons, and the Ladies' Lochs nearby where Victorian ladies might fish at their convenience. In those days there was a much-loved laird, Sir Samuel Scott, who with his wife lies buried beneath a cairn overlooking the sea, a favourite conceit with latterday island owners. The road deteriorates and becomes wilder and gives out on a daisy-brilliant patch of machair at Husinish, looking over the sound to the island of Scarpa.

Scarp, as it is always called, is a lovely island, with much of wildness about it (52), and it might lie across a far wider sea than the narrow *Caolas an Scarp*. It is the home of seventy or eighty people, who have succeeded in maintaining themselves in vigour and simple comfort despite difficulties. Although the market for tweed has declined, the menfolk fish lobsters. The crofts are worked in patches of lazy-bed cultivation, only rarely enclosed. The cattle are wintered in, and in spring put out on the eastmost and lesser of the two hills on Scarp, quaintly fenced with stray boulders or even bits of driftwood linking natural rock-faces and screes in a crazy fold, but one that proves adequate. The cows understand the situation and seldom stray to the crops, which in any case the island dogs are enthusiastically ready to protect. The island sheep are confined to the higher hill to the west. All the cultivation is by hand. There are no horses on Scarp and most of the children have never seen a horse. Mr. Dugald Campbell, the present very active schoolmaster, who helps to keep the outboard engines of Scarp in running order, talks of bringing in a light tractor, which would effect a curious transition direct from manual cultivation to the internal-combustion engine. The last of the true blackhouses on Scarp lately ceased to be inhabited, but a number of them still stand, as steadings : some of them built back-to-back with the space between filled-in with earth and stones. Scarp people, like others in the Hebrides, keep "God's

50 Three figure carvings, including an Abbot
and a man in a kilt, in the wall of the tower

51 The pre-Reformation church at Rodil in Harris
ST. CLEMENT'S, RODIL

52 Scarpa, looking across to Hushinish, North Harris

53 West coast of Lewis at Eoropie

time" and ignore summer time. The view from the hill above the village is splendid: little houses and patches of cultivation at one's feet, only a few small enclosures, one trefoil-shaped, stretches of shining sand beyond, then the mountains of North Harris and of the Lewis shore, and all around many islands rejoicing in the blue and green tides, Taransay, Mealasta, and Gasker where the seals suckle their young. Above the shore, unenclosed, is the cemetery, whose stones are pale rounded boulders simply carried up from the beach below and put down at head and foot of the last resting places of the people of Scarp.

At the mouth of East Loch Tarbert there is a low-lying island, Scalpay, about the same size as Scarp, but with almost ten times the population. Up to the last census the population of Scalpay was rising, but there has since started a sharp decline. The people were fishermen, but today there are only four Scalpay boats working. They cannot compete with the powerful mainland boats. No condemnation is too strong for the continued squandering of the priceless asset of our fisheries. Over-fishing, open poaching, destroying of spawning grounds are the rule. If fewer herring are today thrown away at the ports, that is partly because they are thrown away at sea, when the quota is reached. The skipper of an island boat told me he had known above a square mile of sea impassable for the stench of rotting herring thrown away by ring-netters, poisoning the waters. All efforts to have reasonable restrictions applied have been unavailing, blocked as they are by the irresponsible elected representatives of industrialism.

IV

Lewis is the largest and most populous of the Outer Hebrides, with some 25,000 of a population. Yet it is a poor land and has always been the home of considerable poverty. Practically all the people live along the seaboard: there is hardly a sizable community anywhere inland. The heart of Lewis is hardly conducive to permanent residence. Much of it is a vast morass, a great wet plateful of cold porridge. Few places can look so overwhelmingly wet as landward Lewis on a rainy day: moorland and coarse grassland heave themselves out of lochs that form wherever the earth is level enough. For the greater part of the year the dereliction is terrible. Only for a short summer is the time redeemed. And so as might be expected, the sheiling system flourished in Lewis far later than elsewhere, and is not long given up. The sheilings were the little bothies in which the lassies stayed, herding the cattle on the summer pasturage. They milked the cattle where they fed, and one of the girls would take milk back to the township —creamy milk and delicious, for I know no milk so good as that from a hill-fed Highland cow in high summer when the pasturage is rich with spicy plants. In Lewis not far from Callanish I have seen a most remarkable building, being a sheiling of drystone "beehive" construction built within the last hundred years. It starts on the square to allow for wall embrasures for the milk vessels, and comes into a regular rounded superstructure, all of stones overlapping, originally finished off with turfs. A wonderfully neat bield, with its two yard-high entrances and an ingeniously contrived fireplace and chimney. There are ruins and founds of many others, but this is almost the only intact example left of a building form that could probably claim to be the longest sustained in the world. For these beehive dwellings were built in the Stone Age to precisely the same design—as may be seen in sand-buried remains from Eriskay to Shetland: long afterwards they were being built as the cells of the Culdees—there are two in the Garvellochs, but some say these have been partially reconstructed, and others on remoter island rocks, such as Sula Sgeir. They are shown, built as sheilings though looking rather like wigwams, in an engraving in Pennant's book (7). And here at Garynahine is one built just within living memory, to the design of thousands of years syne. This little stone hut has an intrinsic attraction, there is something peculiarly nice about it apart from its interest. It is a work of endearing skill and judgment, with the way the uncomplying irregular stones are made to comply and to shelve across until they meet save for a last small circular hole bridged with flat stones. Now that the protective carapace of turfs has weathered away it seems that the rest will quickly go unless the sheiling of Garynahine is quickly taken into protective custody. Garynahine lies inland from Callanish with its renowned standing stones, great sinister monoliths of a baffling, mind-dulling obliquity (47). Personally, I rarely find these things attractive, only perhaps occasionally against a happy cloudscape. They suggest a mournful perversion of man's pursuit of the divine, a doomed monolithic mumbo-jumbo, without æsthetic justification. It is dry work becoming excited by them, unless for the ultra-fanciful, some of whom have woven theories about Callanish too far-fetched to be funny.

In Stornoway, Lewis possesses the only substantial town in all the Hebrides. Today it is a place with four or five thousand inhabitants. There are still some pleasant douce houses of the early nineteenth century, a few perhaps older, ever liable to deface-ment or demolition to give place to unworthy successors, but the site in an enclosed loch, with a spit of land that makes for a fasci-nating double seafront, has, like so many Scottish town sites, received too little appreciation (55). The greatest attraction is certainly the harbour pool when it is filled with the herring boats that bring to it a gay, smoky, smelly, brightly-coloured life (54). On a sunny day, looking across the boats to the massed rhododen-drons in the Castle policies, Stornoway is rich and effulgent.

The Castle itself is a vast Victorian pile, but it has fine policies with trees and shrubs and lawns. A real crime was committed on the policies in the war of 1939, when the lawns in front of the Castle were wantonly used for the grimmest massing of service hutments, since become the homes of the houseless, making a horrid mess of a public park that offers so pleasant a place of recreation.

There can be no doubt that there are qualities that only antiquity and a sort of organic relationship to the surrounding countryside can give to any town. Stornoway is not a very old town, nor is it a town that has grown out of its countryside. The first effort at its foundation was made during the reign of James VI by the Gentle-men Adventurers of Fife. The native population resisted the Fifers who had come to develop the local resources, especially the

fisheries, and ejected them with a good deal of slaughter. Charles I,
continuing the effort to develop the fisheries, wanted to make
Stornoway into a Royal Burgh, but the strong protests of rival
burghs caused the Charter to be withdrawn, and Stornoway developed slowly, largely peopled by settlers from without, as
indeed it is even today although Stornoway has probably now a
higher proportion of Gaelic speakers than ever in the past. There
has therefore been rather more resentment between the townspeople and the countryfolk than is usual between town and
country; somewhat vexed in recent years by the development of
the Stornoway tweed mills, and the various disputes over the
marketing of the home-made and the factory-made "Harris
tweed".

As a whole, Stornoway people are extremely kind and friendly,
assertive sometimes and intemperate in various directions, being
not very sure of themselves. Many people have remarked on or
written about the phenomenon of the Stornoway weekend, the
contrast between the bacchanalian carousals of the Saturday
night and the Sabbatarian solemnity of the Sunday morning.
Indeed, the drama of the contrast would be hard to overlook. As
a very shrewd citizen put it to me, the trouble with Stornoway
is that there is too big a gap between those who drink too much
and those who don't drink at all, in short, not enough true tem-
perance. It is unfortunate that the only licensed premises in Lewis
are all congregated in Stornoway, so that the country people are
put to the unfortunate shift of cramming their refreshment into
the exigencies of the bus timetable.

Of course, fishermen and sailors add considerable numbers to
the native population. The airport, which before the war was run
by a staff of three, has now a staff of about 150, of whom many
are condemned to an idleness that only great souls could bear
with merit. For long there were eleven policemen kept at the airport gates in this insufferable vacuity—more than in the whole
of the rest of Lewis. It is not, of course, that there has been any
real increase in the air services. The B.E.A. staff remains at three
and suffers from being suspected of responsibility for a fantastic

54 Stornoway harbour, gay with fishing craft

Stornoway on the Isle of Lewis

55. William Daniell's aquatint of 1819 shows a graceful little launch of Stornoway

state of affairs, paralleled throughout the islands, except in Barra where, the landing-strip being the strand, the Ministry of Civil Aviation has no control and can charge no landing dues nor unload its vast army of supernumeraries which condemn services that were satisfactory and profitable before the war to being a constant drain upon the taxpayers' pocket. The island air services once promised, in the days of enterprise and personal initiative, to be a great boon: officialdom has stunted their development and made them hopelessly uneconomic.

Some years ago an American dietician, making a study of the diets of primitive peoples through the world, drew a contrast between the state of health of people living in the Lewis backlands and those living in Stornoway. He was able to show an extraordinary divergence between even members of the same family. Those who lived on the country, on the simple natural foodstuffs of the old Hebridean population, were vastly more healthy and better developed than those living on the imported diet of Stornoway. Unfortunately white bread and canned food have now become normal articles of diet throughout almost all the islands, with a consequent decline in stamina. Advertising and the whole vast sales machinery of industrialism, staunchly supported by food controls, have promoted a general physical decay. The old diet consisted of oatmeal, in the form of porridge and oatcakes, beremeal bannocks, potatoes, fresh fish and meat, some vegetables, and much milk, butter and eggs.

The food was grown under natural conditions. It is interesting to note that when, during the last decade, efforts were made to produce a disease-free potato by crossing the primitive Peruvian plant with improved species, the seed for the latter had all to be obtained from the Isles. Since then, however, industrialism has thrust the poison of artificial fertilisers into these parts whose poor land had remained healthy. The worst danger of the commercial development of seaweed is that it may promote the use of artificial fertilisers to replace the organic manure of seaweed, which will very quickly return the cherished machair to a state of sand.

9*

Outlying from the main stretch of the Outer Hebrides there are several groups of small islands, now all uninhabited. Although I have seen most of these from a distance, I have not visited any of them. They have been admirably described, with reference to their past histories brought up to date, in a recent book by Mr. Robert Atkinson, *Island Going*. The largest and most historic, being much visited and well documented, are the St. Kilda group, lying nearly fifty miles to the west. St. Kilda (62), with the highest sea cliffs in the British Isles, after being inhabited from early days, was evacuated in 1930. The last crofters left the Monach Isles, a dozen miles west of North Uist, in 1943. Unlike the other remote islands, the Monachs are sandy, machair land, showing golden from the Uist coast. The Flannans, or Seven Hunters, are the site of a lighthouse west of Lewis. A wild place, the great waves swept the three lighthouse keepers off the cliff not long after the lighthouse was founded. To the east of Harris the kindlier Shiant Isles were rendered wretched by a plague of rats that occupied them from a wrecked ship. Their name means the "Enchanted Isles" and folk say they are very beautiful. In Martin's day there was still a chapel there dedicated to the Virgin. Martin writes also of a blue stone in the Shiants and makes an interesting, puzzling reference to seeing "a set of table-men made of this stone, prettily carved with different figures". Did he mean by this chessmen? And if so were his examples comparable to those magnificent Celtic-Viking chessmen of walrus ivory discovered in Lewis, the best of them now in the British Museum and others in the Antiquaries' Museum in Edinburgh?

The remotest isles of all are the rocks of Sula Sgeir and North Rona, north of Lewis. Sula Sgeir is a gannet rock, although at present it seems as if the spreading empire of the fulmars is displacing the gannets. It is an awesome place, with a coast of sheer rock difficult to land upon with the swell about it. There is not enough earth to hold a single spring of water. Yet even on Sula Sgeir there is one beehive *teampull* of some far-thrusting hermit. The men from Ness, by the Butt of Lewis, for countless years made an annual expedition, hauling their light Viking-type *sco* sixty feet up the rock after them, since there is no anchorage, and staying for a few days making a harvest of the gannets. They would kill about two thousand and take them back in salt, selling them at a shilling a head, a much appreciated article of diet. North Rona, although bleak enough and with a bad landing, is more emphatically an island than Sula Sgeir, and it has been the home of regular communities. The ruins of the cell of St. Ronan, built in the Dark Ages of a thousand years ago, are adjacent to the ruins of the later chapel, and near those of still later black-houses. Martin writes of the people of Rona in the late seventeenth century: "They have an agreeable and hospitable temper for all strangers; they concern not themselves about the rest of mankind, except the inhabitants in the north part of Lewis. They take their surname from the colour of the sky, rain-bow, and clouds. There are only five families in this small island. . . ." But a plague of rats, the stealing of the island bull by predatory sailors, and the people being unvisited from Lewis for a year brought disaster and the whole population died. Rona was repopulated, but the men-folk were shortly after lost at sea. In the eighteenth century shepherds were introduced by the tacksmen and the remoteness of Rona inspired two minor poets to write one an ode, the other an epic. The last native inhabitant, Donald Macleod, called the King of Rona, left in 1844. Since then the only residents have been the two elderly shepherds, Murdoch Mackay and Malcolm MacDonald, who went there in 1884 in something of the spirit of the island hermits. They went as atonement for a religious dispute. Two efforts were made to get them to return to their homes and relatives in Ness, but the old men refused to leave. They spent their time tending the sheep, fishing and hunting seals, in meditation and reading the Bible, and were entirely happy. But when a boat made the island the following year they were found to have died, the one neatly shrouded in his plaid, the other as he sat by the fireside. They were buried together in their chosen island in the remote Atlantic wastes between the Hebrides and the Orkneys—the Sudereys and the Nordereys.

Chapter

III

ORKNEY

THE Northern Isles of Scotland are immediately and emphatically different from those of the West. Yet Orkney itself is very different from Shetland, and the Western Isles have their own considerable variations. There is, however, no doubt a generic difference between Sudereys and Nordereys not altogether easy to account for. Racial theories are always slightly suspect, and the Vikings for long possessed and liberally peopled the Western Isles. The people of Lewis are reputed of predominantly Viking stock. Orkney again had certainly some early Celtic incursions and a basic Pictish Celtic stock; while in historic times there was a fairly constant stream of incomers from all parts of the Scottish mainland. Perhaps race is less a matter of blood than of *culture*, and the reasons for the dominance of one culture over others in a racial amalgam impossible to explain to precise satisfaction. Climate and geography must exercise a progressive influence over any race, gradually modifying older inherited characteristics. Yet the fact that the difference between North and West is emphatic perhaps makes one overlook certain links and similarities belonging to populations whose comparative isolation has enabled them to retain certain characteristics of the individual in contradistinction to the submerged man of modern materialism. Not that these qualities of intuitive living and personal value are by any means unique to islesmen, only, naturally, they have there had generally a better chance to withstand the fury of British industrialism; and we do see in the different islands contrasting expressions of the same essential qualities.

The primary difference between Orkney and any Western Isle is expressed, very graciously, in the island's capital, Kirkwall. (56)

The Cathedral of S. Magnus, Kirkwall, Orkney.

56 William Daniell's aquatint showing Kirkwall in 1820

57 Typical Kirkwall street, paved right across

58 Old houses near the Cathedral

KIRKWALL

59 Tankerness House, with its sixteenth-century gateway

60 Old houses in the precincts of St. Magnus Cathedral

KIRKWALL

62 St. Kilda: Village Bay and Island of Dun

61 Lazy bed cultivation as practised in Lewis and Harris

There is nothing comparable in the West to Kirkwall, a township with a thousand years of history. It was founded by Vikings as winter quarters for the sake of that little lopped-off arm of the sea, the Oyce or Peerie Sea, formed by the storm-beach called the Ayre at the end of Kirkwall Bay. Here was a safe harbourage, in which the Viking longships, could be hauled ashore, protected from the tides, yet ready for speedy launching. The Kirk from which the town took its name—properly Kirkvoe, the voe of the Kirk, corrupted into Kirkwa, and hence by the perjink and ignorant into Kirkwall—was St. Olaf's, built about the year 1035. The doorway of St. Olaf's is still to be seen built into a house in Bridge Street. It was a century later before Earl Ronald founded the Cathedral dedicated to his uncle, St. Magnus, to the design of his father, Kol. Kirkwall reached the height of its glory in the ensuing years. By 1400 it was one of the more important and even brilliant capitals of the North. To understand this it is necessary to appreciate that in those days Kirkwall was not a remote place but centrally situated upon the northern trade routes. Much trade passed through, going south and west from Scandinavia. Fifty years before Columbus found backing for his expedition the Earl of Orkney had commissioned the Venetian navigator Zenoni to explore the western seas in search of those lands first reached, indeed, by the Viking ships of long before. The Orkneys and Shetlands were still, of course, Norwegian possessions, as they had been since the Viking invasions of the ninth century, although the Sinclair Earls had considerable independence. The islands were returned to Scotland, under the marriage settlement of James III and Margaret of Denmark, in 1468, and the earldom invested in the Crown three years later. In 1486 Kirkwall received its first charter as a Royal Burgh. If, perhaps, the days of its greatest glory were already past, it still had, and surely has, a full and fascinating history before it. In miniature all the life of a provincial capital of the north has been enacted in the old buildings and the streets of Kirkwall. The trades and crafts guilds were formed (their old insignia may still be seen); the grammar school was founded; there was murder and tyranny;

the Reformation and other factions of history made their impact; babies born who afterwards distinguished themselves far furth of Orkney; in the eighteenth century the dances in the Assembly Rooms were all the rage, and there were even local poets to write scurrilous lampoons about social conceits. In miniature it is like the history of Edinburgh itself: and it has never withered away in incurable decay like many towns, nor been blasted by violent and heady expansion like many more. Kirkwall is in short one of the rightest and tightest burghs left in Scotland, and perhaps the best-looking.

This, indeed, can be seen at a glance. Of course, there is the sheer muck of by-law and state-inspired housing on the outskirts, the dreary contemporary contribution. (Upon what wizened skull did the idea of semi-detachment first break? And what clownish technicians made the semi-detached house the rule of housing schemes—almost impossible to lay out pleasantly, in every way less snug and amiable than the terraced houses that make a street? Swedish wooden houses, painted the wrong colours, are now being landed on Kirkwall. And this in Orkney which consists practically entirely of flagstone, a natural-bedded building stone that can be quarried anywhere. In fact, some of the new houses are built of this wonderfully easily handled stone, but unkindly covered with drab cement.) There are other regrettable lapses, the refacing of houses with false-fronts of cement, even some threat of further demolition. But at the moment Kirkwall is still a delight (58).

First and foremost, dominant and gracious, the Cathedral stands in towering splendour. Its precincts are worthy of it: the little houses with their flag roofs, their courtyards and viting pends. The oldest and finest of them, Tankerness House, wears an armorial blazon on a little balcony over the gateway, bearing an inscription and the date 1574 (59). From within the courtyard the balcony can be reached by a stair, and the household watch in comfort and distinction displays of pomp or violence. The houses stand back from the Cathedral forming a piazza, into which at either end runs a characteristic Kirkwall street, paved with flags right across, meandering, with genial jostling houses, some with gables turned to the street, one or two still with courtyards. They have been called, rather ineptly in view of their great antiquity, Albert Street and Victoria Street, anciently and far more graciously the Laverock. The flagstones keep them clean underfoot, and narrowness makes them the safest streets in Britain. Cars cannot swoop down them but must proceed civilly, sharing the gait with pedestrians. As a result people do not get run over in these kindly streets. (I need hardly say that they strike horror in the hearts of Traffic Experts, who recommend that the lovely houses should be pulled down, the streets widened, the traffic speeded up, and the people of Kirkwall exposed to the full risks of Progress.)

There are two ruined castles overlooking the Cathedral. The Earl's Palace (65), with its strong reminders of old splendour, the ruined oriels, the rib-vaulted chapel, the fine, cloister-like vaulted passage to the ground floor, the great hall with its mullioned window, built for himself in the Renaissance manner by the wicked Earl Patrick Stewart, bastard of James V and Commendator of Holyrood, who used the Reformation to possess himself of the Orkneys. The Bishop's Palace is substantially older (64). The site presumably is that on which that wonderful man, William the Old, made his home. William the Old was made Bishop in 1102, and must have come to Kirkwall from Birsay when the Cathedral was consecrated in 1152. After the consecration, William the Old and Earl Ronald made a pilgrimage to the Holy Land. Pious, jovial, and Viking to the marrow, they provided for themselves on the way by piracy, but, the Saga records, not without the good resolve, "Of the booty we obtain we shall give every fiftieth penny to the poor." Earl and venerable Bishop went by sea, but came back on horseback, overland, to see the sights of Europe. William the Old was Bishop for sixty-six years and died in 1168. In 1188 Bjorni or Bjarni, the Skald, became Bishop of Orkney. He was a distinguished poet, author of "The Lay of the Jomsburg Vikings", a man of culture and ability, and used his wealth towards completing the Cathedral. In 1263 after the fateful Battle of Largs, the effectual end to Norwegian domination in Scotland, King Haco retreated to Orkney, and died that winter in an upper room of the Bishop's Palace. The last great Bishop of Orkney was Robert Reid, the founder of Edinburgh University. It was he who built the big round tower of the Palace, overlooking the Cathedral, which, also, he expanded by three bays. He did much for Kirkwall Grammar School and even intended to found a College in the Burgh, but was prevented by death. His death took place, probably by poisoning, in France, while he was returning from witnessing the marriage of Mary Stewart to the Dauphin in 1558. For this Kirkwall Cathedral nearly suffered the fate of so many of our greater churches, for out of spite for the Bishop's share in the marriage of which they so strongly disapproved, the English sent a fleet to Orkney to sack Cathedral and Burgh. Mercifully, after landing their forces, the ships were driven back to sea by a gale, and the discomfited troops were slain by the Orcadians without achieving their aim.

The Cathedral itself is magnificent. Although none of the modern work is good, there is very little of it, and it hardly mars the splendour of the old fabric. Perhaps the most powerful impression is to be gained from above the crossing, looking west, down the mighty array of pillars surmounted by clerestory and triforium that, in their dense proximity of red stonework, give so astonishing a sense of size to what, in reality, is quite a small cathedral (63). The eastern view suffers from some clutter, including a disproportionate but entertaining nineteenth-century tomb to an Arctic explorer, whose figure reclines less in the repose of death than in a voluptuous sleep, a double-barrelled gun by his side. From without the modern steeple is rather unfortunate, being pitched too high, a suddron conceit that replaced the characteristic squat cap destroyed by fire not so many years ago. But the miracle remains that the Cathedral has survived so well. After the Reformation its maintenance for long depended upon the fornication fines imposed by the Kirk Session, and we perhaps largely owe the survival of the great Kirk built by St. Ronald to the prevailing lustiness of the Orcadian people. One curious fact about St. Magnus's is that it still is, and has been since

63 The nave of the twelfth century Norman Cathedral of
St. Magnus, Kirkwall

64 Bishop's Palace, Kirkwall. Bishop Reid's Tower built in the early sixteenth century

65 The Renaissance Palace, built by the Stewart overlord: the Earl's Palace, Kirkwall

before the Reformation, the possession not of ecclesiastical authorities but of the town, having been given to the people when Orkney was ceded to Scotland. Under the illusion that it was the property of the State, the Government made considerable repairs to it in 1845. William the Old's remains were found, but subsequently thrown away amongst the rubbish. The bones and cloven skull of St. Magnus and those of St. Ronald were mercifully not discovered until more respectful days, and are now preserved in the Cathedral. Some funds for the maintenance of the building were provided by a worthy Orcadian, Gilbert Meason, in 1805; and the generous bequest of Sheriff Thoms has provided for its care in recent times.

Kirkwall has remarkably for its scale the character of a city: may they preserve it. The narrow paved streets, old houses humanly tumbling over one another and beautifully stained with age—especially those in the Strynd, that quaint cut leading up past the Cathedral; backyards and pends; bright shops and teeming shoppers. In the long undarkening summer nights the streets have a great mystery of pattern and form. A fine background this for young people to grow up in, displaying the past of their people gracefully about them, living history, with the curious, sometimes almost sinister beauty of a true town. I almost feel as though it were my own background, for it was my wife's and I know it intimately through her youth.

Again, may Kirkwall be preserved and cherished as it should be. Local writers have compiled admirable histories of this most interesting of provincial capitals. There is Hosack's great book; there is Moonie's remarkable study of St. Magnus; there is the research into the old Orcadian language of Norn carried out by Dr. Marwick, late headmaster of the Grammar School and a scholar of international fame. The tradition is still alive. Today there is a promising, active local Art Society; and even the skipper on one of the inter-island boats dashes out with his sketch book each time he passes the particular headland he is painting at the time.

Kirkwall stands on its bay to the north of a narrow neck of the Orkney mainland, the island sometimes called Pomona, from the

Latin description of it. From here the Cathedral tower can be seen far out to sea, even from the Scottish coast. The bulk of the mainland lies to the west. The roads are many and excellent, running through the farmland that the Orcadians have made so fertile by their labours. Still along the northerly road from Kirkwall towards the village of Finstown, miles of moorland are being reclaimed, sand ploughed into the broken-up peat, crops sprouting where they had never sprouted before. So different from the Hebrides where crops no longer sprout where once they grew. The countryside on the whole is flat, with a slight roll to it.

Stromness, Orkney's second town, lies on its sheltered bay in Hoy Sound that leads into the enclosed sea of Scapa Flow (66). Stromness is an attractive place itself, and large enough to provide a healthy rivalry to Kirkwall. It was a great whaling port in its day, and its men sailed to the farthest seas. Sir John Franklin's ships lay in at Stromness before making their ill-fated voyage to the Arctic. Down by the harbour is a handsome building put up during the Napoleonic wars as a rice store: there is a sensible idea of making a new town hall out of it. The main street is not unlike Kirkwall, rather later built, more sib with the sea. The bay is gay and lively with craft on a summer day. Over the Sound the massive hulks of the Hoy hills make an impressive background, as also they do to the two large inland lochs of Stenness and Harray, lying a little back from Stromness. The Two Lochs are separated by a queer, narrow strip of land, where swans nest a yard from the roadway, only indifferently hissing at the inquisitive. Great monoliths stand memorial to ancient ritual, and nearby is Maeshowe,

> " . . . a monstrous bonny thing
> A field upswalled to man's making
> The heart hacked oot
> The black rock preed
> So that the deid might bury the deid.

Maeshowe is very impressive: this great green mound that conceals a beautifully constructed burial chamber. Perhaps the crusading Vikings, sheltering from the snow, who scratched runic graffiti on walls already ancient, though still charnel enough to drive one of their number mad, provide a bridge across the awful vacuity of time that normally makes the prehistoric so meaningless save as subject for academic postulation. With the runes there is a beautiful little picture of a lion. One of the Jorsalafarars, those Jerusalem-farers who accompanied Earl Ronald, and whose names are preserved alike in the runes and in the Saga, has cut a cross in one of the buttresses. Another, love-sick, has recorded, "Ingigerthr is of women the most beautiful": and this may even refer to Earl Ronald's daughter.

Over on the west coast the Stone Age village of Skara Brae is ample enough to give some impression, but the fine old house of Skaill nearby is more pleasing to the eye, a charming little mansion in the Orkney vernacular. North from Skaill Bay, past the tusky ruin of Birsay Palace, the Brough of Birsay is a sweet green lump in the sea, a tidal island reached by a little causeway, with the remains of the Celtic church of St. Peter's surrounded by the foundations of the little beehive cells of the monks. Turning east again, along Eynhallow Sound, one comes to another promontory, Aikerness, lying across a waste of sand, with rabbits underfoot and hovering, calling terns overhead. Here there is the remains of a broch, with a rock-carved well still spring-fed at the bottom of a long stair within it. The broch ruins are all inextricably mingled with those of a Stone Age village and of Viking longhouses. Nearby, the little modern museum is beautifully built of traditional materials, and is perhaps more interesting than its contents.

East of Kirkwall the more northerly road runs out past the airport towards Deerness. It passes by the larger of Orkney's two distilleries, Highland Park, reputed the oldest in Scotland, having been founded in the eighteenth century by one Magnus Eunson, a bootlegger. Highland Park is a famous whisky, outstandingly one of the best of all: a rich, heavy whisky, the malt prepared over fires of pure peat. Deerness is so nearly an island that it is now forbidden to take any more sand from the narrow neck that joins it to the rest of Pomona, lest it should indeed become an island. The other road runs down, now, to veritable islands, right on to them since the construction of the Churchill Road during the 1939 war. This astonishing, but slightly doubtful, causeway, made of enormous cubes of concrete piled mixter-maxter, bridges the shallow sea to Lambs Holm, Glimps Holm and South Ronaldsay. It was built after the sinking of the *Royal Oak* in order to block submarine ingress to Scapa Flow. Its future is doubtful, partly because it is still subsiding and needs constant repair, but perhaps more because the baffled tides are eroding the land on the North Sea side—there is a difference of several feet between them and the Scapa tides, which shows what a tide-race there has been between the islands.

The approach is made from the village of St. Mary's, Holm. (The parish is pronounced Ham, but the little green holms in the sea are pronounced as they are spelt). St. Mary's is a nice village of typical Orkney flag-walled and roofed cottages. Lamb's Holm, across the first leg of the causeway, is a plain little island, once a vast encampment of Italian prisoners. The chapel they built for themselves remains, an extraordinary achievement fashioned out of a Nissen hut, bits of beaver-boarding and all kinds of scrap. The interior is beautifully painted, and the altar rails are of wrought iron that puts most contemporary British work to shame. Outside there is a concrete statue of St. George killing the dragon. The chapel is proudly cherished by the Orcadians, although presumably the Orkney wind and rain will finally triumph.

Alongside the causeway lie dissolving merchant ships, sunk during both wars to make a blockade around Scapa. In fact, all around the Orkneys the sea is curiously untidy with sunken ships rearing ahigh at low tide, their steel awash at high. Some were sunk by enemy action, but most are blockships. They are a curious reminder of the waste of war. But Orcadians were privileged to observe a graphic illustration of the waste of Industrialism's uneasy peace in 1945 when great quantities of military stores were dumped in disused quarries—crockery and cutlery and other things in short supply. They were destroyed because it was feared they might flood the market and discourage the wheels from turning!

Glimps Holm is a second small island. Burray is larger, with two nice old houses, one, the Bu, standing over a large sandy

Stromness, Orkney

66 Stromness, Orkney, looking across to the Hills of Hoy

From the aquatint by William Daniell. 1821

67 Ward Hill on the Orkney Island of Hoy

68 Quoyness, Hoy, looking to the Orkney Mainland

bay facing north and east to Rose Ness, Copinsay and the Horse of Copinsay. South Ronaldsay is a bigger, more fertile island altogether. It has something of a very small town in St. Margaret's Hope, commonly called The Hope, round the sheltered bay to the north. As elsewhere in the Orkneys there have been many chapels here in pre-Reformation days, and it is interesting that three were dedicated to St. Columba and one to St. Ninian, which, as Tudor remarks in his book on the Orkneys and Shetlands, is fair evidence that the original Pictish population survived throughout the pagan days imposed by the Vikings from 872 until their own conversion 120 years after.

Apart from these islands, and little Swona and the Pentland Skerries, the rest of the South Isles of Orkney lie across the Sound of Hoxa, the only deep-water entry to Scapa Flow. Chiefly their names end with the Viking a, simply signifying an island: Sitha, Flotta, Fara, Cava, Risa. Graemsay has the alternative ay form of suffix. Of these, Flotta is the only sizable island. Hoy, which has kept only the y, is much the largest and most distinctive. It is almost regarded as three islands: South Walls, which is joined only by a long stretch of storm beach now causewayed to North Walls, which has an indistinguishable frontier with Hoy proper. The word means the high island and on Hoy are gathered all the substantial hills of Orkney (67). North Walls itself is divided between North Ness on the north side of the big bay of Long Hope, and Lyness, farther north. There is an Admiralty pier at Lyness and a curious conglomeration of sheds, huts and shacks, many still in use, although it scarcely seems likely that Scapa Flow can ever again be an important naval base. Taking the road north one gradually shakes off the war relics, until one sights the great sunken hulks across Hoy Sound, the tide pouring white over their decks. The country becomes increasingly attractive as one comes up Lyrawa Hill, past two absurdly small lochs called the Water of the Wicks and, imposingly, the Water of Hoy. The chief hills rise abruptly now, fine craggy heights, below them the carse of Quoyness (here the o is mute) with little long, low croft houses, flagstone built and partly roofed, partly thatched, looking out over the blue-green dancing waters of the Sound. Never in Orkney do you see the translucent Iona green: however bright the colouring it is always, as it were, thickened with Chinese white. Sea, sky and landscape have, in comparison with the West, this opaque quality. Generally the lines are horizontal, sweeping along, undulating, for almost the whole of the islands are of flag-stone, only Hoy is mainly of upper old red sandstone formation. On a summer day, after a most refreshing sleep on a bed of short springy heather (surely the most comfortable, accommodating mattress in the world), I made a frontal attack, up the 1,500-foot north face of Ward Hill, the highest in Orkney, where most domin-ant hills are called Ward Hill, meaning watch hill. It was quite a breathless climb, a steep pull, then a short cliff covered with sweet-scented rose sedum, then a steep, slightly curving slope seemingly formed of scree loosely tied together within a sort of string-bag of fibrous vegetation. Below me sea and land had been bright with sunlight, but a stiff wind suddenly brought a dense smoky mist bellying round either side of the hill and flowing out across the sky, turning the sea swiftly to a murky grey with little whip-ups of white spray licked by the wind from the surface of the Bay of Quoys, scurrying out over the Sound.

There is a fascinating out-of-the-world croft village, Rackwick, at the back of Ward Hill. The old road to it, past the characteristic Orgill Lodge, is the most Highland-looking part of Orkney. As a road it is quite washed away by the winter rains, with a sandy or rocky bottom, winding through heather, flirting with burns, one making quite a deep cutting with rowans and bushes along it, Western Isle fashion. Rackwick is a green place, with old houses and the odd Nissen hut, beyond it some magnificent pink cliffs and the celebrated pillar rock, the Old Man of Hoy. Hoy is, of course, the poorest of the Orkney agricultural land and scantily populated. It is the last substantial estate left in the islands, a beautiful and strange place with a rich bird-life. Amongst its flora it claims a patch of the intensely rare *Primula Scotica*, found only in a few places in Orkney and Caithness and Sutherland, and never surviving transplanting.

The northern islands of the Orkney group lie scattered, flat, like bits of a jigsaw puzzle, or, seen from the air, like the map on one's knee being made manifest in earth and water. The inter-island boat sails from Kirkwall to visit most of them, varying its run according to the tides, usually lying overnight in Westray before making the return trip the following morning. It is a homely, friendly trip, with no very long crossings. Shapinsay, which lies just across from Kirkwall Bay, is a regular day jaunt for the townspeople in the summer visiting the grounds of the nineteenth-century Balfour Castle. Stronsay, farther out and to the east, has the remains of a considerable herring station, deserted since 1914, with large disused sheds beside the landlocked har-bourage of Papa Sound. Only occasional fishers put in now. A good many of the houses here are now empty and roofless, but all so neat and clean that they give little sense of decay. Round the bay the solid, douce two-storeyed houses stand, many dated 1905, 1906, 1907, progressively, but breaking off short when the herring industry departed. Even the gentlemen's lavatories by the pier are built of the flat natural flagstone, and somehow look so much more agreeable for it. Inland the soil is particularly fertile and well farmed, and Stronsay has still a population of six or seven hundred. Papa Stronsay that helps to enclose the harbour is one of a number of Papas in the Orkneys and Shetlands, the name signifying the home of priests of the Celtic Church.

To the north lies the flattest and farthest-stretching of the islands, Sanday. Sanday is very flat indeed, and sometimes from a boat the houses seem to be standing in the sea. It is commonly and aptly compared in shape to a lobster for the way it straggles. A plain enough island on a hazy day, when the sun bursts out it is transformed, brilliant with greens and blues of intruding sea arms, the charlock gleaming yellow, and the good houses manifesting themselves, lit up. Besides good houses, Orcadians keep good tables. I think I've had some of the finest meals of a lifetime in a rambling old farmhouse on Sanday. Fresh lobster with home-made mayonnaise, served with bere-bread that used to be standard fare through most of the north but is now practically confined to Orkney. Not for Orkney the dreary, wrapped, flavourless white bread imported to the Isles of the West, or the incessant white flour. Bere is the "unimproved" barley, four rows of grain to an ear; it is milled in local water-mills and made into a satisfying brown, almost purple-brown, scone, excellent with meats. A word must also be said of the dropscones, which I only enjoy made by an Orkney hand. Eggs and chicken, fresh fish, fresh butter, and dense broths complete the glories of a simple fare treated with a proper care.

Sanday has been the scene of many wrecks, once considered as a source of providence. Sir Walter Scott records a Sanday farmer replying piously to Stevenson of the lighthouses who had remarked on the tattered state of his sails, "If it had been His will that you hadna built sae many lighthouses hereabout, I would have had new sails last winter." There is a lighthouse across the shingle on Start Point, the eastmost tip of the Orkney group. Even so, remains of wrecks litter the sea around Sanday. Across the sandy, rabbit-ridden, pleasingly named Plain of Fidge stand great radar masts, some partially dismantled. An ex-Homeguards-man told me how he and his companions, after a celebration, once sportingly climbed to the top of one of them.

Beyond Sanday lies North Ronaldsay, much the remotest island of the group, having only an occasional boat service. Before the late war it had a regular air service. An old lady of eighty taken from North Ronaldsay to hospital in Kirkwall, while quite at home in the familiar aeroplane, refused to travel in a car, never having seen one before, and a pony and trap had to be procured to take her from the airport into Kirkwall. North Ronaldsay is renowned for its sheep, little, dark, Shetland-type beasts, kept *outside* the dyke that encloses the island from the shore. They feed chiefly on seaweed, and the mutton is said to be excellent, though I am sorry to say I never tasted it.

West again from Sanday lie Eday and the Calf of Eday, Fara and the Holm of Fara, then Westray with Papa Westray which has its own Holm of Papa. It is at Westray that the North Isles boat lies at the pier to the north of the Bay of Pierowall. Coming

69 The ancient round-towered church on Egilsay, Orkney

70 Ring of Brodgar. Standing Stones of Stenness, above the
Loch of Harray, Orkney

71 Arctic Skua

72 Great Skua

73 Arctic Tern

74 Red-throated Diver

<small>On their Nests</small>

157

75 Prehistoric dwellings excavated at Jarlshof, Shetland

76 Shetland ponies on the Island of Mousa, with the remarkable
broch in the background

inland, past an upper-room teashop, modest and concealed, and a little shop proclaiming simply "Remnants, Fancies, etc.", one comes to a pre-Reformation chapel that retains its chancel arch, all its windows square-headed, and two fine seventeenth-century grave slabs lettered in high relief. The ground rises attractively towards Noltland, pronounced Notland, Castle, a huge imposing edifice of various periods, but in some part dating from Scandinavian days. So remote a castle, yet no other in Scotland so bristles with defensive precautions. The enormously thick walls are riddled with shotholes, even piercing the angles. The very yard-wide newel of the stair is a concealed sentry box. The steps of the great stair are seven foot long, ten foot at the angles. Even in ruin it is a fascinating place. It was burnt by the Hanoverians of the '45. Today fulmars have started nesting on the windy tops of Noltland. There is a nice walk beyond it, over moorland blue with little scillas, to cliffs clamorous with sea-fowl, and back again by the pale sands of the links, the Castle rising grandly beyond. Although the population is reputed to have fallen to a half since 1900 when it stood at 2,200, Westray is still intensely farmed after the Orkney fashion. It has some primitive houses, the Orkney variants of the blackhouse, all of flagstone, with a wisp of thatching at the top. The stones are the size of the peats in the stacks by the doors, quaintly like them, except that they are paler in colour.

South from Westray, within ferry-distance of the mainland, Rousay has the most interesting contours of the North Isles. A series of hills, enfolding a couple of lochs, slope down to the shore. At Hullion there is as good a group as you will see anywhere of traditional Orcadian houses, walls and roofs all of a piece, all of flagstone meetly descending a slope, quite beautiful like such a group in Northern Italy. Alas, the flagstones are now being stripped from roofs throughout Orkney, and horrible synthetic asbestos replacing them, dull, garish, mechanical. Even those who want to replace their flags cannot do so, for the ministry of cheese-paring works will not give them licences for strong enough timbers. It is impossible to believe that a Government busy founding Arts Councils and the like has really got an idea as to what culture is when it shows so little care for the essential simple things, the æsthetic background to our living from which springs so much potential joy. One would like to see the Orcadians showing their wonted independence and cherishing the exteriors of their homes as much as they cherish the interiors.

Between Rousay and the Mainland lies Eynhallow Sound, called after the little green holy isle that lies so daintily halfway across. Eastwards are Wyre and Gairsay on which stands an irresistible little seventeenth-century Orcadian mansion, with its courtyard and ornate curtain wall. This is a house of the type that inspired the later Professor Lethaby to build Melsetter in Hoy, a house whose design has latterly been so much admired by architects in the south. It is said that Lethaby, having drawn out plans for Melsetter before visiting Orkney, was so much impressed by the traditional style on his first visit that, despite his client's protests, he insisted on completely changing his original plan, and based the present plan on those lairds' houses and large farmhouses that were built with their steadings around courtyards, replacing the midden with a rose-garden.

Egilsay lies along the east coast of Rousay (69). It is a sweet green island, approached on the west side by a pier built dry of flagstones atilt, herringbone fashion. The track from the pier passes through a ruinous steading, the population being now much reduced, partly, it is said, through lack of a good boat service. Beyond stands the remarkable church with its chancel and round, Irish style but not free-standing, tower of inscrutable age. Some have dated it from Celtic days, others from after the conversion of the Vikings, others, again, put it as a later rebuilding than the church in which St. Magnus prayed before his martyrdom. On the knoll nearby where, traditionally, Hakon slew Magnus, there is now a monument, sensibly built of flagstone save for a concrete cope already cracked: it was put up by the parishioners of St. Magnus in Kirkwall and St. Magnus Martyr in London. The church of Egilsay is a charming place, so nearly intact and now well kept, grey stone with yellow lichens, the land falling smoothly from it down to the sea. I was there on a sunny day, while one of the regular Orkney

organised picnic parties, this consisting of émigré Egilsay folk from
distant Kirkwall, disported itself, and little boats plied across from
Wyre and Rousay, their crews coming for the football and the dance
with which proceedings were to be brought to a proper close.

That is all too brief a summary of islands that, not being very
spectacular, have more charm to them than is easily conveyed.
They were first described in post-Scandinavian days by the almost
anonymous "Jo Ben", who seems to have been a priest and may
have been called John Bellenden. He visited the Orkneys, it is
said, in 1529, but for some reason it is thought to have been rather
later, and is a kind of equivalent to Dean Monro who travelled
the Western Isles at the same period. His account is interesting
enough, but brief : it would seem he found the people not naturally
religious but inclined to superstition. In Stronsay he cured a
lady who had a monstrous lover covered with marine plants.

The Orkney Islands have today a population of some 22,000.
Yet, like the Western Isles, depopulation is steady : some little
holms are already deserted. No one can say it is poverty that is
responsible for the decline in Orkney : the people are uncommonly
well off. The turnover of exported eggs runs to a million pounds a
year. Some misgiving as to the future of poultry-keeping (perhaps
a too credulous belief that the Government would indeed conjure
its eggs from Africa) has stimulated something of a switch-over
to bacon. Everyone everywhere seems to be building pig-styes
and buying and selling pigs of all ages, with substantial profit all
round. People live in great activity and comfort. Why the depopulation? As one who has failed to be convinced in an ineluctable progress towards an inevitable mediocrity, I cannot accept
that Orcadians drift towards the millenium. I think it is easy to
underrate the tremendous power of suction of a centralising
machine such as has been evolved with particular efficiency in
Britain : propaganda declared and undeclared; films with their
horrible dream-world of material ooziness; wireless and great
sections of the Press; so-called education—all consciously or
unconsciously play the same pipe-tune, luring to fatuity. There is
a deadly machine that has come to shape our ends.

Chapter

IV

SHETLAND

THE Shetland mainland stretches north for nearly sixty attenuated miles; a long, thin backbone with water-ragged projections to east and west. The airport is on the Links of Sumburgh, at the southern tip, always a centre of some population and point of some contact with the world beyond. At Jarlshof—a romantic name applied to the old mansion by Sir Walter Scott, and still sticking—are the remains of the houses of the men of the Early and Late Bronze Ages (75), of a broch, of Viking longhouses, of the seventeenth-century mansion of the Bruces of Sumburgh, with a Victorian mansion, and then, to the north, the airport itself. A long tradition of man's tenure. To the west rise the dramatic high cliffs of Fitful Head. From Sumburgh the main road runs north, keeping to the east of the backbone of low hills. Beyond the bay of Leven Wick, Wick being a Norse word always signifying a bay up which boats could be drawn, side roads lead to Sandwick, a disused copper-mine, and the handsome old house of Sand Lodge. Across a narrow sound from the Lodge lies the island of Mousa, a pleasant green isle and far-famed for having on it the one example of the mysterious broch that remains to us near-complete (76). Mousa being one of the few parts of Shetland geologically akin to Orkney, the broch is built of flagstone, and was no doubt preserved from the common fate of other brochs, that of being used as a quarry, because there was plenty of suitable stone available for such other building as ever was done on Mousa. It is an astonishing place, this truncated cone of stone, still rising over forty feet, grown slightly ogival with the sag of age. Within the wall, which is fifteen feet wide at the base, the staircase spirals, with access to galleries growing narrower until the top one

77 Gables turned to the sea: old street houses in Lerwick

78 Lodberries, houses built out into the sea on piers, the old form of landing-stage at Lerwick

becomes impenetrable to a man of average size. Nobody really knows anything whatever about the manner of living in brochs, though Mousa had what must have been two of the last occupations. Two runaway couples took shelter there: one the Viking, Bjorn Brynulfson, who eloped from Norway with a lassie called Thora about the year 900, and stopped for some winter weeks in the Broch of Mousa on his way to Iceland. The second was also a Viking, Erlend Ungë, who had gone off with or, some have it, been dragged off by Margaret, Countess of Atholl, a widow much older than himself. Concerning the original inhabitants and even the precise purpose of the brochs, all is conjecture—although presumably they were defensive, but erected by whom against whom? Archæologists seems to get more angry with each other about brochs than they do about anything of which something definite is known. Were they originally roofed, and, if so, how? Were the galleries residential, or purely constructional? What are the little interior windows for? To gaze down from the ramparts of Mousa into that funnel of piled stone almost without history is to look at a building more completely in another lingo than anything else I have ever seen. Ordinary conventions of window and stair do not apply. It is impossible to visualise the unrecorded first inhabitants: yet they must have been an astute and able enough people with no mean sense of architecture, and they left a lovely blank wall for the graffiti of archæologists.

The wall of Mousa has today been plugged and propped by the Office of Works with injections of cement, but not visibly, and the flags are yellow and green with lichens. A small drove of Shetland ponies trots about the greensward of Mousa under the broch, old mares casting their coats like blousy ladies in moth-eaten furs, and foals very dainty following. The flag rocks recline at an easy angle of repose towards the circumambient sea. An old man used to work at them, making flags for the streets of Lerwick, but dull concrete is now replacing the flags there.

Lerwick, the Shetland capital, lies a dozen miles to the north on a harbour given shelter by the Isle of Bressay. It hardly looks as big as Kirkwall, but, with 5,000 of a population, is larger. It is a vertical town, charging by little alleyways down a steep slope to the sea, and, as though carried on by the momentum, houses stand right out into the sea. These houses, called lodberries, are built on piles at the south end of the town (78). They were the original piers, some dating from the eighteenth century. Ships unloaded at their sea-doors and the cargoes were brought in, it is said, by two entrances. One, official, for the customs men to inspect, and a second, a passage through the foundations going under the roadway to the houses opposite, convenient for contraband.

The steep alleys with their stairs and garden walls, with even, sometimes, leaves hanging over them where some tree has flourished in a small way in the shelter of the houses, give a great character to Lerwick (77). Needless to say there is some move to clear them away, and the lodberries too, to reduce all to dullness: may they survive until good sense prevails. The lodberries incidentally are doubtless good wind and sea breakers. When some fine old harbourside houses were demolished in Kirkwall, their absence was found to be a great disadvantage in the winter weather.

The causewayed streets of Lerwick are like Kirkwall's, but, although there are wider streets, the total effect is different, with the sense of the vertical, of an amiable crampedness, and a pressure concentrating on the big busy harbour. Even today one may sometimes hear the sound of sabots and see Dutch sailors clattering unremarked through the Lerwick streets. There are waterside cafés with photos of Antwerp and Amsterdam on the walls, and good meals reasonably priced: friendly places with the right quality of the cosmopolitan to them. On a good summer day the harbour is gloriously lively with men and boats, bright paintwork and silver-sided fish, gulls patterning the air with white curves and the earth with weaving shadow. Herring pour out in silver streams; huge, valuable halibut are hoisted ashore. Fishers and curers and buyers, old salts, small boys, and casuals cast expert eyes upon every activity. Steam and smoke and smells fill the overcharged air. Only, of course, the fishing is getting worse. The last two years have been bitterly disappointing. The wild Shetland winter threatens bleaker when the summer earnings are so thin.

To allay that long relentless winter Shetlanders have quite recently developed a pageant without parallel in Britain. Up-helly-A is not, properly, an old festival: not like the Christmas and New Year Ba'games during which excited Kirkwallians hurl themselves into the harbour, while shopwindows are barricaded. The burning of a tar-barrel at the end of Yule in Lerwick a hundred years ago does not even seem able to claim the very respectable antiquity of the Burghead Clavie. But out of it has been developed a true spectacle, elaborately and completely organised, a classical formula designed for the full release of romantic spirits. Long winter months of brief days are redeemed by the planning and making of elaborate costumes, magnificent or grotesque, done in secret by each of twenty or thirty squads, with ten or twenty guizers in each squad. A full-size model of a Viking longship is built with as much care as it put into the building of any boat for the sea. On the last Tuesday in January the Viking squad of the Guizer Jarl bring out their ship. The hundreds of torches are set aflame at one signal, and an elaborate, carefully marshalled march takes place through streets crowded with people from all Shetland. Bands play, there is marching and counter-marching, rockets are fired from the Fort and the ships in the harbour. Down at the wharf after a burst of song the flaming torches are tossed into the galley. But the night goes on in a dozen dance-halls, every one of which each team of guizers is expected to visit. Here the womenfolk have prepared entertainment and refreshment for the heroes of the evening.

Only a pundit could complain of the lack of heredity of a fiesta that so completely justifies itself every year. Indeed, there is something impressive in the capacity shown by the Shetlanders to create something new in a very short time at a period when most creations are ephemeral and superficial. Up-helly-A has the human tradition that is the justification of old things.

Another Lerwick speciality is the natural zoo of Noss. If its range of exhibits is small, and somewhat seasonal, its creatures are all wild and free. The expedition is made by ferry-boat to Bressay, green like much of Shetland, but perhaps a misleading, infertile green. On the west side are well-kept crofts, but on the east mostly larochs until the road descends sharply on to the swift-flowing strait between Bressay and Noss. The shepherd resident in the one house of Noss ferries visitors to the natural zoo: the only four-footed creatures sheep and rabbits, with presumably less visible rats and otters. The real exhibits are the birds. First perhaps a pair of graceful-flying Arctic skuas (71), Scootie Allans, as they are called, for their unpleasant habit of scaring the vomit out of gulls and catching it neatly in mid-air. They are most irregularly piebald below, with curious projecting central tail-feathers. Then the great skuas, the bonxies, start upon one from their nests all up the slope to the Noup (72). As one comes into each nesting preserve the bonxie lofts itself with an indignant noise like crunching gravel, poises, draws back its wings, and plunges at one's head, customarily just missing it, but it is almost impossible not to be perturbed as this large bird projects its weight at one's hat, often from in front, sometimes from behind or sideways, suddenly and unexpectedly. Occasionally they stoop at the numerous rabbits, but in mischief rather than determination, for the rabbits generally ignore them.

Along the low cliffs the fulmars glide from their nests in the earthy places, almost the most graceful fliers of all birds, gliding without wing-beat, rising and falling with no apparent effort. Sitting on the water they look rather silly, pigeon-like; but in the air they are inimitable. On the surface of the sea eiders swim with the rare ducklings that have survived the bonxies and greater black-backed gulls. Then one comes on the first puffins, sitting like red-nebbed diners-out with large yellow boots, scudding with unbecoming, hurried wingbeats to the sea surface. They are grotesquely human and seem to fly like a man might fly, in vast doubt, trailing big boots through the air, apprehensively looking over his shoulder; and the bonxies and black-backs catch them in scores and empty out their little feathery hides and leave them all over the grass. Coming up to the Noup of Noss itself the cliffs grow grander and more densely peopled. Young gulls hirple along the tops, finding holes to hide in. A wall has foundered,

79 A typical Shetland croft

80 Shetland croft in the snow

81 The northernmost tip of Britain: Saxavord Hill and Burra Fiord
from Petester, Unst

82 The fine profile of the loneliest of the Shetland Isles, Foula

bulged and collapsed with the changing levels of the breaking cliffs. Greater black-backs sit in a sinister ring around a huge cauldron. Just below the Noup one comes on the best show of all, the gannetry. A great stink of rotted fish rises from the trails of cream-coloured guano beneath each nesting niche. And niche is all, often seemingly sloping only outwards. One grows dizzy watching and wondering how the fluffy baby gannets remain in place. The old birds feed their young and each other and bill and possibly coo, but one can distinguish no separate noise from the noise of innumerable birds sounding like the buzz of a hive of immense shrill bees, a shapeless noise, with just a fringe noise of wheepling oyster-catchers and gulls. The gannets, with some tysties (black guillemots), sit so densely that one feels that a careless wingbeat could brush off a whole community.

An easier, less exact and exacting outing is by the steamer from Lerwick that sails under the Noup and lets cry with its siren, causing the whole cliff-face of birds to rise in one alarmed mass.

The simmer dim is what they call it, the darkless Shetland summer night. One sees it from the window of the high hotel where they feed one so well, looking out over lums and masts and funnels, water unexpectedly unruffled, Bressay beyond. Reds, greys, blacks, and yellows of the fishing fleet, gleaming white of the new *St. Ninian* and the North Isles boat, the *Earl of Zetland*; white and dark yachts with masts fragile against the sea. Bressay a lustreless green with still bright patches of charlock. Still a few gulls scavenge the paved streets. Into the quiet the resonant chimes of the Town Hall clock strike an unreal midnight.

Sailing in the *Earl of Zetland* for the North Isles on a fine summer day is a good gay experience. One comes out of Bressay Sound by the gleaming dark-bright coastline. Be it remarked that the Shetland light is quite unlike either the translucent light of the Hebrides or the white, opaque light of the Orkneys: it is, as far as one may describe it, a dark, a black, or a blue light, that seems to reflect the North. Often, of course, all is haze. Although the Shetland rainfall is not high at 38 inches, the rain takes a long time in falling, rarely coming in the torrents of the Hebrides,

11*

but a small rain, making for frequent cloudedness. Bright sun-shine is rarer and warmth less than in the Hebrides. Indeed Shetland, with an average maximum temperature of 48·8° Fahren-heit and an average minimum of 40·8°, has the most equable temperature in Britain. But it is palpably less warm in summer than anywhere else. When the sun is bright it is bewilderingly bright, usually emphasised by dark clouds standing back, and making Shetland exceptionally photogenic.

Out from the Shetland mainland south of Whalsay there is a remarkable chain of little reefs of gneiss with jovial names: Hoo Stack, the Sneckan, Little Billan, Muckla Billan, Muckla Fladdicap, Rumble, they form an almost straight line running north-east and terminating in the Out Skerries, which last for all their remote rockiness are the home of a flourishing people renowned for their physique, fishermen. Whalsay itself is dominated by the sub-stantial granite house of the Bruces of Symbister, now flanked by some "non-traditional" imports. A flitboat, as the ferries are called, meets the steamer, which then, if one is lucky, sails for the Out Skerries, where about a hundred people live and thrive. Even for Shetland they are sea-conscious and boat-minded, small boys dexterously catching and making fast ropes flung to the flitboat from the steamer: even smaller boys rowing confidently in the graceful Shetland boats, such small boys as would nowhere else be allowed to handle a boat bigger than the little toy boat that these mariners tow behind a real boat. The Skerries are very lovely on a good day, separated by rockbound lagoons—there is no sand. The houses for the lighthouse keepers' families are now in ruins, having been badly blitzed during the war, twice bombed.

North of the Skerries lies Fetlar. As one sails, suddenly the familiar trail of white gulls breaks up into startled screaming individuals, dispersed by a massive dark, sinister skua like a devil loose amongst foolish angels. Herring gulls and kittiwakes are favourite prey of the bonxie: it is afraid of the greater black-backs, and the oil-squirting fulmar it leaves severely alone. Even the gannet, biggest of all our seabirds, is not safe. A friend told me he had twice seen a bonxie wear down a gannet, forcing it to alight on the sea, edging towards it, seizing its wing, turning it over, drowning it, and eating heart and liver as it lay on its back in the water. Yet the tiny tern seems, almost always at least, to be a match for the skuas. One sees the tern rounding on its aggressor, its beak going like a little hammer-head pivoted on long strong wings, screaming its fury, and supported by a flurry of its mates. (Indeed, the tern is more likely to draw blood from the human transgressor of its nesting-place than is the bonxie.)

Fetlar was one of the few parts of Shetland that was cleared of people for the sake of sheep in the last century, and today, although a fertile place, hains hardly two hundred people. It has a big bay to the south; here and to the east live most of the population. The mansion, Brough Lodge, is now left somewhat lonely on the rolling green ground to the west. It is a quaint, happy folly of a house, a sort of original box with an observatory built like a tower on a neighbouring knowe but linked by sundry walls; with a laundry in the guise of a chapel with belfry and stained glass. Small, deserted islands, some used for grazing, lie in the waters enclosed on three sides by the north of Fetlar, the long flank of Yell, and the south of Unst where it enfolds Uyea, which has a house or two and the ruins of a chapel.

Unst is the northernmost island of the Shetland group, a sur-prising place, plain in parts and most simply beautiful in others, full of variety and unexpected things (81). To geologists it is a constant source of delight with the profusion of the formations through its twelve-mile length. Chromate of iron was long mined here, but supplies seem to have given out. Some of the serpentine, a dark blue, lies in piles by the pier at Baltasound beside white heaps of soapstone or talc, crumbling softly, soapily between the fingers, still exported for making talcum powder and the like. Even gold has been mined, but rather as a whim, and there are traces of platinum.

Unst, which comes within four hundred miles of the Arctic Circle, has a feel of Ultima Thule about it, a kind of recklessness, an ending, and many cheerful people ready to laugh. And always it has been a full stop, with its ancient burial-places, immemorial legends of giants, names left by Vikings—as the bay of Harolds-wick, where Harald Fairhair landed in 875 to add Orkney and Shetland to the Norwegian crown. In the black days of Orkney and Shetland history, the days when the thugs of the Reformation came predatory from Scotland with Earl Stewart, bringing bloody oppression, Lawrence Bruce, a half-brother of Robert Stewart, built the northernmost of their notorious castles at Muness in the south of Unst. An interesting little castle, for all its bad history, it is unfortunately a ruin now, though its fine knocker still knocks on the door of Sand Lodge.

Balta Sound is in fact a bay, sheltered and so named because the island of Balta lies across its mouth. By the pier stands an unfamiliar wooden church, a Swedish church served by a Lutheran pastor in the summer months for the many Scandinavian fishing boats that put in at Unst. Nowadays they are chiefly Norwegian harpooners catching sharks for the livers. I am told that Norwegian small change is accepted in the shops of Baltasound. Norway indeed is within equal sailing distance from Unst as Aberdeen, and so is far less remote from Europe than the southerner tends to think. I was in Baltasound for one of the regattas that are the chief sporting outlet of Shetlanders. Football is played a little, regularly against Orkney, occasionally against the Færoes. But the summer regattas taking place off the coast of every substantial village are the occasion of all real excitement and enthusiasm. The Shetland models, sixareens, sail either with a single square sail, which has to be lowered at every tack, or with sails fore and aft. They are the most beautiful of small craft, locally made on principles pronouncedly Viking: double-ended, the clean sterns make them faster and far more graceful than comparable craft from the south. They are built to a lovely curve, enabling them to heel over with hardly a keel. It was an unforgettable sight watching them beating up Baltasound in a sunny breeze. Up on the hillside an old man told me the form of all the boats, and although he com-plained that his sight was failing he seemed to see far farther than I. Down by the pier sports were held, bairns racing and jumping and stimulating themselves with lemonade out of the bottle. A fishing boat towed the fourerns out for the pulling race, four men and a cox in each, and it made one sore to watch their darg.

A concert and dance conclude the second day's racing. Unlike the Hebrides the Shetlands have no songs of their own and fall back, not very appropriately, on Irish songs, with occasional Aberdeenshire ballads: *The Rose of Tralee* followed by *The Mucking of Geordie's Byre*. It is curious this lack of native singing in the Northern Isles. There must have been songs; there was never any censorship of them such as was suffered by the Gaelic, yet today there is nothing. The Up-helly-A song is a Victorian jingle. There are scarcely even any old rhymes, and the stories and legends are very sparse compared to those in the West. Here is one recorded in the last century and plainly dating from pre-Reformation days:

"Mary Midder, had de haund
Roond aboot for sleepin baund,
Had de lass and had de wife,
Had de bairns aa der life.
Mary Midder had de haund
Roond de infants o wir laund."

And here is a guddick, a riddle on the snowflake:

"Fleein far but fedderless,
New come oot o Paradise,
Fleein owre da sea and laund,
Deein in me haund."

In both may be noted the Shetland accent hardening *th* into *d*, which is never heard in Orkney, where "thu" replaces the Shetland "du" for "thou". There are some curious surnames common only to Shetland, such as Hoseason and Herculeson. The reason for them is that, as in Wales, surnames are comparatively recent, while the old Norse names, being deemed pagan by ministers of the eighteenth and early nineteenth centuries, were deliberately corrupted into Biblical and, strangely enough, classical names. Thus Osie became Hosea; Hakon became Hercules; and both duly received their suffixes.

From Baltasound the road runs north by Haroldswick, forking east to the northernmost village of Norwick and west to the farthest north tip of Hermaness, with the last bit of inhabited Britain, the lighthouse of Muckle Flugga, lying off it. Hermaness forms one side of one of the loveliest of the Shetland voes, Burra Firth, of which the east side is completed by Saxa Vord, a substantial hill of nearly a thousand feet. The best approach is not from Haroldswick but to the west, along the ridge by Petester. From here one gains a superb view looking down the curving freshwater Loch of Cliffs, hardly visibly separated from the Firth itself, to the headland of Saxa Vord and the great pink cliffs, blue-shadowed above the sea. On the surface of the Loch of Cliffs the immature bonxies, not yet mating, gather in evil congregations of a dozen or more, like a lot of horrid witches and warlocks plotting cruelty. The little kittiwakes come in, so pretty except for the nasal accent with which they cry their name, to wash the salt from themselves in a small annexe to the loch, horribly near their ruthless enemies, and looking innocent and defenceless as they hover like snowflakes.

Hermaness indeed saw the salvation of the bonxie. Here in 1904 there lived what were reputed to be the last two or three pairs of great skuas in the world (72). Thereafter they were preserved and have now increased to probably undesirable numbers, doing great slaughter amongst other rare birds. Hermaness is thick with them: after passing through various stages of vexation one becomes almost unconscious of their dive-bomber swoops at one's head. Young birds are at first rather attractive in their dun fluff, save for an unkind beak, but they grow plainer. Right in the midst of them on a small tarn I found the two eggs of a redbreasted diver, dark-brown camouflaged against the mud: one wondered how they could survive in the skua country. There are a few scootie allans too, indulging aerial bickering with their bigger neighbours; and it was they who destroyed a whole family of merlins in Hermaness about the time I was there.

It is not to decry Noss to say that the Noup cannot compare with the bird cliffs of Hermaness. They are difficult to reach. One looks down the steep slope of crumbling rock and loose earth and

can see no likely descent. Far below I watched a delightful under-
water game played by a seal mother and her pup in the sun-clear
sea. Eventually the mother seal nosed her pup up a rock on which
a shag was drying its wings, splashing the laundry and sending
the shag, indignantly protesting, waddling up the rock. But there
is a way down if one is shown it. What a world one finds at the
bottom amongst the enormous sloping slabs of dismembered
cliff. A bird world, peopled, denizened, bedizened by birds:
sitting, nesting, screaming, flying, feeding, swimming. On all
sides towering rocks with patches of brief turf and sea-pinks: cut
off from mankind, save for occasional glimpses of the impersonal
lighthouse of Muckle Flugga. But around, all birds. Puffins like
ourselves trying to fly, anxiously winging over the terrifying
depths, frock coats and flat feet flying behind; then sitting on
rocks with a cluster of slippery sand-eels for the bairn in its
burrow. Razor-bills, sleek black-and-white, faces finely marked,
big beaks, sit quiescently within one's reach, turning their heads
from side to side. Guillemots sitting row on row on the rock
perches: mostly eggless and youngless (eggs fallen off? blown
off by the big gale? eaten by bonxies?), only one or two with large,
bonny spotted blue eggs between their little feet. Fulmars in
gloriously isolated nesting-places. Then the gannets, huge,
creamy-headed, black wing-tipped, in great ivory clusters, with
black-beaked, fluffy young. Kittiwakes close below one as one
peers over high rock tops, yellow-beaked and red-mouthed,
affectionately nestling their young, or flying gracefully and
squabbling. Occasionally a great skua flies round, prospecting,
and is driven off by a greater black-backed gull jealous of his
larder. All this in high summer, for birds breed late in Hermaness.

There is now an overland route back to Lerwick from Unst, by
bus with ferryboat hops between Unst and Yell, and Yell and the
Mainland. Yell is the largest of the lesser islands, a solid mass of
peat-covered gneiss. It is rather sparsely populated, the main
centre Mid Yell, properly central at the narrow waist between
Mid Yell Voe and Whale Firth. At the south end there is a
pleasant group of voes and freshwater lochs. An unexpected escape

grows by the roadside, a large, handsome leafy plant with a cluster of daisy-heads, spread from seed brought home by a sailor: they call it the Australian Daisy, but some say it is Indian.

The northernmost part of the Shetland mainland is desperately nearly a separate island itself, linked only by the green ayre of Mavis Grind where the North Sea waters of Sullom Voe all but burst through into the big Atlantic bay of St. Magnus. It may have been due to clouds but the North Sea certainly looked less bright than the Atlantic when I visited Mavis Grind in the summer of 1950. I was in the company of two busloads of Professors and Scholars attending the Viking Congress in Lerwick that year. Having been told that it was possible at Mavis Grind to throw two stones from the same spot so that one fell into the Atlantic and the other into the North Sea, I initiated a ploy that was promptly taken up by the whole party, to the jeopardy, the distance being just great enough and Professors not commonly adept at stone-throwing, of many of the better brain-pans of northern Europe. But at length most of us achieved the feat.

Beyond Mavis Grind lie the parishes of Northmavine and North Roe and the chief hill of Shetland, Ronas, a long, lolloping stretch rising a little less than 1,500 feet above the red rock shore of Ronas Voe. Here was one of the Norwegian whaling stations, now closed, not popular with the Shetlanders, for it was thought that the waste discouraged the herring. It was the seabirds who loved the waste, becoming so entirely dependent upon it as to lose their skill at fishing, so that when one whaling station closed down they died in hundreds on the hillside. With the Viking Congressmen I was nobly entertained by the people of the little village of Hillswick, who were even able to provide addresses of welcome in Danish, by a young girl working there, and in Norwegian, by a native who had married and settled down. West from Hillswick lies the Atlantic promontory of Eshaness, the far bound of St. Magnus Bay, a bonny place of green turf prancked with wildflowers, cliffs wonderfully worked by the sea with arches and gullies and the Holes of Scraada. The Holes of Scraada, though now there is only one hole, the intervening arch having

83 Cliffs on the west side of Fair Isle

84 The landing stage, Fair Isle

caved in, like the Gloups in Orkney, consists of a sea entry through a tunnel only reaching daylight again at the bottom of an inland pothole, with appropriately interesting noise and effect. In winter storms the noise is said to be like gunfire, and the green grass of Eshaness is in places covered with stones thrown and blown right up the cliff on wave and wind.

The other side of St. Magnus Bay is formed by the big promontory south of Mavis Grind that prevents the mainland from being altogether attentuated. It runs out to the Sound of Papa Stour, a once priestly island renowned for its caves. Fifty years ago at Flemington, in the comparative shelter provided by this bulk of land, the local doctor established plantations of sycamore, willow, elder, larch and Scotch firs. His house remains with its garden embowered in these woods, utterly different from any other place in Shetland. South of Flemington lies the fine Voe of Weisdale, picturesque seen from the road above it with successive strips of water lying beyond. The road winds round the top of Weisdale Voe down by Tingwall Loch. Here on a little island, made into a peninsula by an old stone causeway, the Shetland Viking *Thing* held its meetings and made its laws a thousand years ago. I was there when Professor Sveinsson of Reykjavik gave an oration in Icelandic, which is almost identical with the old Norse language last spoken there hundreds of years before. From Tingwall it is a short distance to Scalloway and the substantial ruin of the Stewart palace, "built with blood" in 1600 but hardly lived in, so quickly and neatly did James VI oust Earl Patrick. Scalloway is a nice seaside village, with one very fine old panelled house embellished with a coat of arms in high relief, now somewhat neglected (85). Norwegians were stationed here during the late war, and one Christmas, unable to get a Christmas tree in Shetland, sailed to their enemy-occupied country and brought back a tree.

A thousand Christmases earlier another Norseman, called Naddod, champing to get home to Norway for the Yule feast, left most of his companions behind in Lerwick and sailed his longship into such a storm that it made him the discoverer of Iceland. Lerwick lies just across the narrow girth of the mainland from

Scalloway. Although both Harold Hardraada and Haco sailed
from Lerwick to their respective defeats at Stamford Bridge and
Largs, Lerwick is not really an old town like Kirkwall. It was
simply a place that proffered safe harbourage, and there was
some scandal attached to the first planners for its improvement
who built crude drinking dens for the Dutch sailors at the end of
the sixteenth century. It was Cromwell building his fort to keep
off the Dutch who virtually founded a town at Lerwick. The
Dutch later partially destroyed the fort, which was rebuilt at
the end of the eighteenth century and given the name of Fort
Charlotte, and Lerwick was erected a Burgh of Baronry in 1818.
Although about of an age and a size with Stornoway, Lerwick
seems far better integrated with its countryside. It is, of course, a
county town. But we cannot overlook the curious fact that the
people of the North Isles seems more naturally adaptable to town
life than the people of the Western Isles. The reason, I suspect,
is not racial (Lewismen, as has been remarked, are predominantly
of Norse origin), but geographical, due to some inexplicable
characteristics of climate or what would you?

Before the 1914 war Lerwick harbour used to be solid with
fishing boats during the season. Now the fishing has greatly declined, and the knitting, which for some four hundred years
has been the ancillary to the fishing, is suffering from the unkind
stupidity of the Welfare State that prevents the Shetlanders from
having first claim on their own wool. Shetland women are the best
and fastest knitters in the world, and native Shetland wool is
renownedly soft and light. There are few left now who can knit the
finest work of all, those lovely lace shawls whose four square
yards of intricate and varied patterning weigh only some three-
and-a-half ounces and can be drawn without harm through a
wedding-ring. The wool is plucked from the necks (Shetland
sheep are never clipped, but plucked, "roo-ed") of pure-bred
sheep, now usually from Unst. It must be specially spun and can
only be knitted by a woman with soft hands, often, therefore, by
a cripple unable for housework. They are surely the summit of
the knitter's craft. Besides the coloured Fair-Isle patterns, now

slightly degenerate in design, there is very pleasing knitting of natural coloured wools, from the five varieties of fleeces, white, black, grey, dun, and moorat.

Shetland has two remote dependencies; Foula (82) far out to the west, and Fair Isle (83, 84), almost halfway to Orkney. Without a boat of one's own, or time to wait for the next steamer, both are hard to visit, although now, perhaps, there is not the same need of the solemn warning given by Mr. Tudor in his, as may be judged, remarkably complete guide to the Orkneys and Shetlands published in 1883. ". . . a word of caution," writes Mr. Tudor. "No one should land on any of these islands, when there is a chance of being storm-stayed, or it might be, though rarely in ordinary summers, weeks, without a pocket enema, as alteration in diet, and what not, are apt to bring on violent constipation, which purgatives seem at times to increase instead of dispersing. One or two lives might have been saved here, and in Foula, had this simple means of relief been within reach." Sea-birds were the traditional diet of Foula and Fair Isle. One sees the imposing cliffs of Foula from the west mainland, second highest in Britain only to those of comparable St. Kilda. Fair Isle one looks down on from the plane, spreadeagled green on its cliff top. A great place for migrants, it is now a bird sanctuary and observation post, sensibly run with good accommodation for visitors.

Today the total population of the Shetland Islands is a little less than that of Orkney, rather under 20,000. It is surprising it should be so large, for the land is chiefly pretty barren. But the people are extremely hardworking and enterprising, the men natural seafarers. Many of them who have hardly set foot in England have served for years on the whaling ships, spending their days in the Antarctic. Like the Orcadians, the Shetlanders tend to feel less concerned about religion than do the Hebrideans, although perhaps, their life here being less certain, they care rather more than the Orcadians. Shetland is the chief stronghold of Scottish Methodism, and there are chapels of various denominations in Lerwick, with a Catholic church served from Orkney for the Irish herring-gutters who come in summer.

12*

OTHER ISLANDS AND
A CONCLUSION

I

OF the islands of Scotland outside the main groups the best beloved and most intimately known to visitors is certainly Arran. Arran is likewise the largest of these other islands and the noblest, with its great mountains rising to 2,866 feet, higher than any others in the south of Scotland, rugged, dramatic, with famous rock-climbs. It lies far south, indeed a little farther south than Berwick-on-Tweed, in the enclosed waters of the Firth of Clyde, on the routes plied by the Clyde steamers.

For fully a hundred years now Arran has been a popular resort, but with visitors who respect and cherish its amenities. It has been happy, furthermore, in its landlords, the family of the Dukes of Hamilton, who have owned Arran for nearly five hundred years and are now represented in that ownership by the Duchess of Montrose. There are few houses in Arran that are not let for the summer months: many of them have an annexe or cottage to the back into which the owners move holus-bolus to make room for the visitors. Those visitors customarily return, year after year, to their chosen island, where they find peace and wildness, looking to stretching waters bounded by indented coasts and far mountains.

There are three bays on the east coast served by steamers from the mainland piers: Brodick (86), whose castle was so often demolished and rebuilt between the times of Bruce and Cromwell; Lamlash, the most sheltered bay, protected by the thousand-foot high massif of Holy Island, but with its pier at present out of

86 Brodick Bay, popular amongst visitors to Arran

87 Millport, the township on the Great Cumbrae

88 Bute, looking from Ettrick Bay to the hulk of Arran

89 The wild Atlantic coast of the Shetland mainland

99 The Cumbraes and the hills of Arran from the Largs shore

commission; and Whiting Bay to the south (96). From Brodick and Lamlash roads cut across, making short cuts to the ring road that circles the island and keeps to the coast, save for a stretch along the north tip where cliffs bring it inland. The mountains are grouped in the northern half, but the south is nowhere very level, although more tractable as farmland. Arran is so wild and free, not tamed by the rows of douce villas along its bays, that it is a little surprising to cross the road from Brodick, up the steep brae called The String, and down to the coast at Machrie, and look across a narrow, gentle sea to the long low coast of the Mull of Kintyre. Even there are trees on this west coast, somewhat wind-flattened above Machrie Bay, but beyond, more sheltered yet, including palms growing with apparent contentment. To the south are caves, amongst them the one which is reputed to have been the home of the celebrated moralising spider of Robert the Bruce.

Arran's companions in the Firth of Clyde are Bute, with its dependency, Inchmarnock, which combine with Arran to form the County of Bute, and the Great and Little Cumbrae, close into the Ayrshire coast (90). Like Arran, Bute is a popular resort, but with a different clientèle, the emigrants from the denser homesteads of Glasgow, coming away for some alleviation, but not too much, still liking to feel the pressure of other people around them, cheery, friendly, distrustful of solitude. As a result, despite a vast annual immigration, Bute is remarkably un-spoilt (88). Once one gets away from the recognised centres, Rothesay with its gay but awful Clyde-resort architecture, the piled, tasteless buildings and absurdly beckoning vulgar shops, and the fine sands of Ettrick Bay lying to the west, once linked by tramway, now by bus, to Rothesay; once one gets away from these and from one or two other outcrops of houses, one can wander through pleasant rough Lowland country, seeing hardly a soul even on a hot hazy day in the height of summer. The Firth of Clyde is a wet part of the world, and when it is fine it is rarely clear but with a shimmering diffused light, a homely light for the crowds of trippers on the familiar steamers: "Guid sailor—me? I could sail doon the Clyde in the cabin end o' a whelk!" It is the

traditional Glasgow relaxation, patronised with pride and determination. We may see its beginnings recorded on tombstones in
the ancient churchyard of St. Blane's: the carter of 1805 becomes
the carriage-hirer of twenty years later. Already the Glaswegians
are repairing to Bute, grander people no doubt then, but founding a
tradition inherited by the humblest. Edmund Kean, the actor,
was an early visitant, building himself the delightful villa that
still stands amongst trees above a neat round green lawn sloping
to the shore of Loch Fad, unfortunately not setting an architectural
fashion that was followed in the locality.

Not that Bute's history begins with the incursus. St. Blane's is a
Norman and early-pointed church on a Culdee foundation, a
pleasant place amongst sycamores and whitebeams with a terraced
churchyard and a peaceful, grassy monastic track winding to
Kilchattan Bay. Rothesay Castle itself is particularly interesting,
although only visible from close-to, so hemmed-in is it by houses
advertising "Kitchen To Let"—which means a bed-kitchen. It
was perhaps founded in Viking days by Magnus Barefoot, certainly part dates from the time of Allan, High Steward before
1230. Subsequently it was added to, and subtracted from, until
it stands as it does today, an interesting, elaborate, moated building, newly presented to the Nation but still under the hereditary-
keepership of the Stewarts of Bute. In 1778 the first cottonmill
in Scotland was built at Rothesay, a handsome factory later run
by David Dale, father-in-law of the humane Owen. It still stands,
now a tweedmill producing excellent materials.

Millport, on its open bay on the Great Cumbrae, is a less hectic
township than Rothesay, its houses chiefly older and dis-
creeter (87). It also is a resort for Glasgow folk. It has the Episcopalian "Cathedral of the Isles", a quaint but pleasantly and
piously decked-out, foreshortened piece of Victorian Gothic, with
a "College" alongside it. It has also an aquarium with bright
blue lobsters, horrid hermit-crabs, fancy starfish, huge dahlia
sea-anemones, and little girls exclaiming "Here's a guid yin!"
The Little Cumbrae has an important lighthouse with radar
equipment and, facing the mainland, a nice little square tower

looking to its opposite number on the Ayrshire coast, a watch-tower of earlier times. To the south, the green granite, curling-stone rock of Ailsa Craig rises, a familiar hump off the Ayrshire coast (98).

II

Altogether the Gazetteer credits Scotland with 787 islands with one or other or both of two qualifications: either having enough grass to sustain one sheep, which includes many uninhabited isles, holms, and green rocks; or being inhabited, which includes grass-less rocks that support a lighthouse. Apart from the major groups, nearly all the lesser isles lie along the sea-torn West Coast, off the shores of the Highland counties of Argyll, Inverness, Ross, and Sutherland. To the extreme north, Caithness has one island, little Stroma, a stepping-stone to the Orkneys. To the extreme south, Galloway has four or five small islands in the Solway Firth, besides the Scar Rock farther out where gannets have lately started to breed. One of these Galloway islands, Ardwall Island, which is actually tidal, unlike its two neighbours, the Murray Isles, was the first I ever visited. I went to it several times as a small boy, gathering brambles amongst dense tangles of under-growth and beneath clouds of pestiferous flies. The occasions were always organised picnic parties, functions that I never liked, but, despite all exacerbations, I felt a glory about being on an island, even an island too filled with weeds and elders-and-betters and that tamely linked itself to the mainland by a strip of muddy sand at the ebb-tide.

Down the whole length of the East Coast the only islands, the Black Isle being merely a courtesy title for a fertile peninsula and the Bell Rock an apt description of an infertile reef, are those in the Firth of Forth. These number ten all told, and one can memo-rise their names as one can memorise Latin nouns:

> "Inchgarvrie, Mickery, Colm, Inchkeith,
> Cramond, Fidra, Lamb, Craigleith:
> Then round the Bass to the Isle of May
> And (thrown in to complete the verse)
>   past the Carr to St. Andrew's Bay.'

Small islands—the biggest of them, the May, is little over a mile
long—they have no history as independent units with their own
populations, but link their past to that of the mainland about them,
the Lothians and Fife. They maintained in turn monastic settle-
ments, garrisons and prisons, and now lighthouses. The May
was once a royal rabbit preserve, then its Benedictine priory was
a place of pilgrimage, again patronised by royalty. Some time
after the Reformation it did have a village life, of a rather irregular
kind, a home for Fifers avoiding the press-gangs, for smugglers,
and wreckers who had the active assistance of the lighthouse
keeper. This phase presumably came to an end shortly after 1730,
the last date on a tombstone in the old churchyard. Earlier, Sir
Andrew Wood brought off two of his naval triumphs against the
English "off the May". To the south the fine sea hump of the
Bass Rock (1), whitened by its gannetry, corresponds on
the Firth of Forth pretty exactly to Ailsa Craig at the mouth of
the Firth of Clyde.

Most of them being rarely visited, again it is rather as part of
the Firth, patterning and making various the surface of the waters,
that the islands are appreciated. Only one of them is the object
of regular outings, on a minute scale compared to the trips "doon
the watter" of the Clydefolk. There are summer trips to Inchcolm
(which means Columba's Isle, but not that he ever visited it)
from South Queensferry, also from the Fife shore. Inchcolm is
the most interesting of the islands, for much of the Priory remains (91), the tower and the chapter house and the quaint
cloisters, bare walls tunnelled by slitted openings (92). It can be
very charming on a good day, the ruins above the bay, not mean-
inglessly ruinous, and left peaceful once the bulk of the trippers
have gone off to find picnic sites. There remains even, although
at some date it has been somewhat reconstructed, the cell of the
Cludee hermit who gave shelter to Alexander I for three weeks
when he was shipwrecked on Inchcolm in 1123, in thanksgiving
for which he founded the Augustinian monastery on the island.
Quite a distinguished place, Inchcolm, where the greater part of
Fordun's *Scotichronicon* was written actually by Walter Bower,

91 The Monastery founded by King Alexander I in the thirteenth century
on the island of Inchcolm

92 The little cloisters of Inchcolm Abbey

93 The Castle, Loch Ranza, Isle of Arran

94 The narrows at the Kyles of Bute

95 Glen Sannox, Arran

96 Whiting Bay from Knockankelly

97 Arran from Ardrossan

98 Ailsa Craig

Both after aquatints by William Daniell (1816–17)

Abbott during the first half of the fifteenth century. It is also featured in *Macbeth:*

> "Sweno, the Norway's King, craves composition;
> Nor would we deign him burial of his men
> Till he disbursed at St. Colme's Inch,
> Ten thousand dollars to our general use."

One tombstone alone remains of those and the cross that marked the burial-place on Inchcolm of Sweno's Vikings.

Inchcolm suffered various assaults from piratical English vessels, but Inchkeith, to the east, was held for a year or more by an English force which included Italian mercenaries until on Corpus Christi Day, 1549, the French and Scots stormed their stronghold and triumphed in an extremely bloody battle. Inchkeith has a bad coast, but its water was, of old, considered the best, being longest-keeping, for seagoing vessels to ship. The very small island of Inchgarvie had its fortress, and now supports one leg of the Forth Bridge. Cramond Island is tidal, linking with the shore at Cramond village. Nearby Inchmickery, whose Gaelic name means "Isle of the Vicar", may have had a hermitage occupied from Inchcolm: it used to have excellent oyster-beds, unfortunately spoilt by over-dredging. Fidra lies off the East Lothian coast near North Berwick, connected to the shore by a rocky reef called the Bridge: it had a convent on it. Near Fidra are the even lesser isles of Craigleith and Lamb.

III

Those who visit the Islands of Scotland must have, or cultivate, some indifference to wet weather. The weather is absolutely unpredictable, which is a good thing, since it no doubt preserves islands of exquisite beauty from ever becoming mere hedonist playgrounds. I used to say one could count on February and August as always being wet months, and then in one year we had a February rainfall of ·05 inches, and an August of more than three solid weeks of brilliant sunshine and intense heat. For some reason the Hebridean sun can burn the skin quicker than almost any other and needs to be absorbed with discretion. But visitors must go to the Isles without expecting sunshine or they may be disappointed. For the visitor to the Isles of the West it is essential, too, that ideas of clocking-in, punctuality, and the like should be left behind in the Cities where they belong. It is not merely a matter of quaintness and unpracticality but of a different tempo of life and one that, if not so fashionable, is at least equally relevant to the good life. I would say more relevant. Crofters are often miscalled lazy. There are lazy crofters as there are lazy everything else, but the average crofter is far from lazy. If he is willing to stop work and talk for half an hour, or an hour, that is his recreation, and a more charitable and less silly one than going to the cinema. He makes up for it by working till sundown. Generally he has work in a true proportion: it is not a slice cut out of his being himself, but, with everything else he does, part of his being. What fine sensible, good-natured housekeepers the womenfolk are. Testament to their capacity for humane hard work is the excellent nurses they make. A reflection upon the lack of understanding of Welfare Governments is the fact that they should lavishly endow hospitals with equipment and overlook the more important essential of personnel. For years the Isles have provided nurses of prodigious humanity and capability, but little has been done to ensure the continuance of this supply. The fast-dwindling island populations cannot long continue to provide those admirable nurses, sailors, policemen, to reinforce our national life. These "invisible" imports from the Isles are not reckoned when their value to the commonweal is decried. There is a sanity, a capacity for calm, amongst the islesfolk that has been of untold value to our country. Unfortunately it is not easily transmitted to their children if these are born and brought up in urban desolation.

There are two possible principles for dressing against island rains. Visitors too often make the mistake of trying to compromise with the uncompromising. It is useless to take ordinary townee mackintoshes and so-called stout shoes. Either one must make oneself genuinely impervious with the best of oilskins, preferably the untearable type, and with big, solid, greased boots, or else let oneself get thoroughly wet and be prepared to change. Rubber boots are useful enough for plowtering around but not for long walks. Mackintosh trousers likewise are tiresome. A kilt is the ideal garb because it is easy to get an oilskin long enough to cover it, while stockinged legs do not get unpleasantly wet. For footwear I have found low-cut crepe-soled sandals most practicable, somewhat akin to the light leather brogues of the old days. They are light and easy to walk in, get a grip of rocks, and let the water out almost as fast as they let it in. Really heavy boots are likewise comfortable, but if they are not watertight they fill unpleasantly with wetness. It is the half-way footwear, not heavy enough, that is most tiring and impractical.

All islands are surrounded by water, but not all the waters are equally negotiable. Those keen on boats need to pick their shores or they may find themselves faced even on calm days with ugly swells. Otherwise, of course, and particularly for the practised, the Isles offer perfect sailing, in their variety of coasts and crossings. Fish fresh off the line is to many nowadays a new experience in gastronomics; forby there is all the fun of catching them, fun if you are not too particular about comfort.

Living on islands for those not born to it can be a major experience. But it must be done as living indeed, not as an escape or a charade. Properly lived it is an escape from escapes, from all the bric-à-brac that we too readily assume is living but in fact is mainly distraction. It is to gain a new focus by which things, by losing an old, overbearing importance, can show more freshly to our rediscovered independence. Of venue in its concentration and isolation it is the nearest thing to recapturing a country childhood. "In country children, especially," remarks Dom John Chapman, "the mind is not so full of images, the reason is not yet working at full energy, the soul is receptive, therefore, and quiet; the faculty of perceiving pure truth is not yet wholly atrophied. The experience is imperfect and not in the least understood. In older life it will perhaps be totally forgotten. Yet it seems likely that such a child will never become a convinced materialist (except perhaps in words), but will always *know* (without reasoning or feeling) subconsciously that there is a beyond."

Islesfolk are not a pack of saints, they share the universal ills, but remoteness and the inevitability of being often alone, and quiet, do give them a chance, too rare in a predominantly urban population, to live with eyes looking beyond the world. They may seldom be able to put words to what they see, but it is immanent in their capacity to act intuitively. They are, after all, in some part heirs to the hermits who built their rude *teampulls* on stark rocks and who had a much better apprehension of what life was about than do the sociological dreamers of today, with their plans for "bringing the Isles into step with Modern Progress."

Map of Scotland

showing the chief islands

5 10 5 0   20   40   60   80   100 miles

SHETLAND ISLANDS

Foula I.

ATLANTIC

Fair Isle

OCEAN

ORKNEY ISLANDS

NORTH

Lewis

Shiant Is.

Harris

Moray Firth

HEBRIDES

N. UIST

S. UIST

SKYE

Raasay

BARRA

RUM I.

EIGG

MUCK

SCOTLAND

COLL I.

TIREE I.

Staffa

MULL

IONA

COLONSAY

SEA

JURA

ISLAY

Firth of Forth

Glasgow

Edinburgh

KINTYRE

ARRAN

Firth of Clyde

Ailsa Craig

IRELAND

Solway Firth

ENGLAND

I. OF MAN

Flannan Is.
or Seven Hunters

Carloway

Uig
Breascleit
Callernish
Stornoway
Eye Peninsula

Aird Bhreidhuis

L E W I S

N O R T H

Loch

SCARPAY

L. Langabhat
L. v.Shimid

M I N C H

Scurst
Amhuinnsuidhe

Tarbert

Shiant Is.

H A R R I S

Sound of Harris

Haddachuan

Heisker
Is.

LITTLE

Duntulm
The
Quirang

Gairloch

N. UIST

Loch Maddy

MINCH

Ascrib
Is.

Monach Is.
Shillay
Lighthouse
Ceann
Ear I.

Boreraig

SOUTH
RONA

BENBECULA

Dunvegan

Applecross

Portree

RAASAY
I.

SOUTH UIST

Talisker

Sligachan

SCALPAY

Kyle of
Lochalsh

Cuillin
Mts.

Glenelg

ISLE OF
SKYE

Sgurr
Alasdair

Glamaig

Kyleakin

Loch Boisdale

Loch Brittle

ERISKAY

SOAY

Sound of Sleat

CANNA I.
SANDAY I.

BARRA I.

Castlebay

RUM

Allival
Askival

Mallaig

Sgurr nan
Gillean

L. Morar

MINGULAY
BERNERAY

EIGG I.

Arisaig
Pt.

Barra
Head

MUCKL

Loch
Shiel

Ardnamurchan
Pt.

COLL
I.

Tobermory

Loch Linnhe

TIREE I.

ULVA

STAFFA
Fingals
Cave

Ben More

Oban

IONA

Ross of Mull

Easdale
I.

SEIL
I.

The Hebrides

0   5   10 15 20 25 30
miles

SCARBA

COLONSAY

JURA

The Shetlands

0 1 2 3 4 5   10   15
miles

Muckle Flugga
Herma Ness
Holm of
Harolds wick
UN
Ballasound
Balta
Ham of Muness
Uyea

Uyea
Fugla Ness
YELL
FETLA
Hascosay
Head of
Lambhoga
Ronas
Hill

Grind of the Navir
Rocks of
Scradda
Tangwick
Hillswick
Dore Holm
The Drongs
Lamba
Brother I.
Lit.
Roe
Bigga
Samphrey
linga
Lunna Ness

ST. MAGNUS
Mangaster
out
Skerr
Egilsay
BAY
Brae
Muckle
Roe
WHALSAY
East
Linga
Papa
Stour
Vementry

SHETLAND

Vaila
Tresta

N. Havra
Sanga
Stour
Loch of
Tingwall
LERWICK
BRESSAY
Isle of Noss
Noup of Noss
Hildasay
Chenies
Oxna
Trondra
Scalloway
Quarff
Holm of
Noss

FOULA

West Burra

South Havra
Ness of Ireland
Mousa
St. Ninian's
Isle

Fitful Head

INDEX

The numerals in **heavy** type denote the figure numbers of the illustrations.